LOLA

CAN-AM AND ENDURANCE RACE CARS

DAVE FRIEDMAN

FOREWORD BY
JOHN SURTEES

MBI Publishing Company

First published in 1998 by MBI Publishing Company, 729 Prospect Avenue, PO Box 1, Osceola, WI 54020-0001 USA

© Dave Friedman, 1998

All rights reserved. With the exception of quoting brief passages for the purposes of review, no part of this publication may be reproduced without prior written permission from the Publisher.

The information in this book is true and complete to the best of our knowledge. All recommendations are made without any guarantee on the part of the author or Publisher, who also disclaim any liability incurred in connection with the use of this data or specific details.

We recognize that some words, model names and designations, for example, mentioned herein are the property of the trademark holder. We use them for identification purposes only. This is not an official publication.

MBI Publishing Company books are also available at discounts in bulk quantity for industrial or sales-promotional use. For details write to Special Sales Manager at Motorbooks International Wholesalers & Distributors, 729 Prospect Avenue, PO Box 1, Osceola, WI 54020-0001 USA.

Library of Congress Cataloging-in-Publication Data

Friedman, Dave.
    Lola: / Can-am and endurance race cars / Dave Friedman.
      p.   cm.
    Includes index.
    ISBN 0-7603-0646-X (alk. paper)
    1. Lola automobiles--History. I. Title.
TL215.L65F75   1998
629.228--dc21   98-34964
                          CIP

Edited by Zack Miller
Designed by Tom Heffron

On the front cover: John Surtees on his way to winning the 1966 Times Grand Prix at Riverside. Surtees would go on to win the Can-Am championship that season.

On the frontispiece: Night-time wrenching on the John Mecom Lola T70 at the 1965 12-Hours of Sebring. Mecom's car was driven by John Cannon and Jack Saunders.

On the title page: A. J. Foyt (83) and Parnelli Jones (98) dice at the 1966 Times GP at Riverside. Unfortunately, both drivers retired early due to overheating.

On the back cover: Top: Mark Donohue had a brand new Lola T70 Mk. 3 to race in the 1967 season. This shot was taken at Las Vegas, a race Donohue would go on to win. Bottom: The Bonnier/Axelsson (11) Lola leads the Locke/Bailey (14) Porsche 906 at the July 1968 Watkins Glen 6-Hour Race. The Lola coupe went on to finish 10th overall.

Printed in Hong Kong through World Print, Ltd.

CONTENTS

	FOREWORD	6
	PREFACE	7
	ACKNOWLEDGMENTS	9
CHAPTER 1	LOLA MK. 6 ARRIVES, 1963-1964	11
CHAPTER 2	THE GLORY YEARS, 1965-1967	37
CHAPTER 3	NEW LIFE AND A DOWNHILL SLIDE, 1968-1970	93
	COLOR GALLERY	97
CHAPTER 4	FADE TO BLACK, 1971-1974	145
	EPILOGUE	159
	INDEX	160

FOREWORD

Dave Friedman, a name synonymous with photographic artistry, has captured motor sport history as it was created, particularly on the tracks of North America.

For that reason it is highly appropriate that he should create a record of a marque that had such influence on American sports car racing, and at times dominated some of the classes in which it competed. That marque, Lola, is one of which I have many fond memories as well as the odd nightmare.

My first connection with Lola cars came in 1961 when I called at the small workshop in Bromley, two streets away from where I lived, to meet Eric Broadley and Rob Rushbrook. Theirs was a complementary relationship, Eric expressing an idea or putting it on paper and then Rob creating the actual car. I was just coming off my first full year in motor sports, a rather disappointing season in the production Formula 1 Coopers that Yeoman Credit—managed by racing legend Reg Parnell—had acquired.

I believed that to gain more knowledge, to match the speed I already possessed, it would be good to be involved in the development of a car— for Yeoman Credit and myself to function as a works team. That works team would be the Lola's first entry into Formula 1. Though I did not win a Grand Prix, I did come second and third, sit on pole position, and win nonchampionship races. An astounding record for a first-year effort.

From there I moved on to Ferrari, but at Eric Broadley's request—and with Ferrari's blessing—I got involved in his new T70, the racer Broadley had penned after selling the first Lola GT project to Ford. I agreed to carry out testing and to race the T70 in selected events when my Ferrari program allowed. We chose Chevrolet engines from Traco to power the new car, and, after some brief sorting, we were competitive in both England and North America.

The low point in this winning relationship came when I had a horrendous accident at Mosport. I had formed a two-car team to contest various events, and I was driving the newly built second car in practice. I had won at Brands Hatch shortly before at the wheel of this new T70, but for Mosport it had been allocated to Jackie Stewart. He had voiced some complaint, and when I went out to check it, the car lost a wheel. When I came to in the hospital, Rob Rushbrook told me that it was not a Lola-built part that had failed, but a part that had been supplied by and inadvertently fitted to the car by the American agent who was discussing an agreement for manufacturing the models in America.

I recovered from my accident, but not in time to drive the Lola Indianapolis car on which I had carried out development testing for Broadley and George Bignotti. While lying in the Canadian hospital, I had to offer my advice regarding who might take over my Indy ride. I suggested Graham Hill, and as history shows, he brought Lola its first of many Indianapolis wins.

Once healthy, I started preparing to challenge the inaugural Can-Am series of 1966. It was to be a low-budget affair, a Chevy van, a trailer, a T70, two Traco engines, and Malcolm Mallone to drive the van and prepare the car. After a hard-fought series, we ended the season victorious.

The following year brought another Lola milestone that I was able to assist with. I had joined Honda, and to speed development I suggested a cooperative venture between Tokyo and Lola cars. When this finally came together, personnel from Lola and Honda put their heads together, along with myself, to create a new version of the chassis that I had helped develop for Indianapolis. Thus was born the Honda 301, built in conjunction with Lola, which went on to win the Italian Grand Prix.

Unfortunately, the 1967 Can-Am program did not go so well as the Honda venture. At the end of the season I finally borrowed back my old 1966 winning car and engine and ended my Can-Am Lola career with a win at Las Vegas.

History shows Lola's influence in Can-Am diminished as its main rivals, McLaren and Chaparral, received the backing of General Motors. Then Porsche arrived with its turbocharged projectiles, and suddenly all the rules changed. These corporate-backed developments drove the series into big-budget racing and obsoleted small, independent manufacturers like Lola. But at Can-Am's dawning it was Lola that was dominant, and though its winning ways would wane as the series matured, its early influence would be reflected in the cars that would later inhabit the winner's circle.

—John Surtees

PREFACE

Between 1963 and 1974, the end of the Can-Am era, many of the world's most famous drivers drove a Lola at one time or another. From 1965 to 1967, when the Lola T70 was in its prime, virtually every top driver in the world, with the exception of Bruce McLaren, Chris Amon, Jim Hall, and Jim Clark, drove one.

Much of the Lola's technical story has been told in the books written by Ian Bamsey (*Lola T70 V-8 Coupes*), John Starkey (*Lola T70*), and Pete Lyons (*Can-Am*), who remains the dean of Can-Am writers. Lyons also covered many of the Lola's technical details in his outstanding six-part series on the Can-Am in the old *Vintage Motorsport* magazine.

One of the shortcomings I find with some of the sports car histories coming out of Europe is their light coverage of the history those cars made in North America. After all, the vast majority of the Lola T70's history and many of its important victories happened in North America. I've attempted to address this lack of North American history by creating a good overall photographic history of the American-engined Lolas and the people who drove them. *Lola Can-Am & Endurance Race Cars* is full of unpublished or infrequently seen photographs, accompanied by extensive quotes from those who were involved with the cars at the time they were raced in anger. Whenever possible, I selected photographs showing more than one car. There were so many great cars and drivers racing during the Can-Am era that I wanted to incorporate as many of them as possible in relating the story. I know that I have not succeeded in showing all cars and all drivers, but I think you'll be pleasantly surprised by how close I have come. I also think you'll be intrigued by the number of outstanding drivers, from all types of racing, who drove the Lola and by what many of them have to say about the cars and those very special years.

In putting this book together I culled a photographic collection of more than 600 images down to the 250 best presented in this book. Most of the photos are from my collection, but I've also called on some of my photographer friends to round out the story. I hope you'll be pleased with the result. Enjoy!

ACKNOWLEGMENTS

This book could not have been done without the backing, encouragement, and enthusiasm of the publishing staff at MBI Publishing Company. As always, I must thank Tim Parker, Jack Savage, and Zack Miller for their help in making it all happen.

Susan Claudius corrected my grammar and spelling errors. Susan also has a way of bringing to my attention all of the words that I have left out of my sentences. It seems, for some reason, that my brain goes much faster than my pitifully slow typing fingers. Many thanks also to John Surtees who took time away from his busy schedule to write the foreword to this book.

I cannot begin to thank all of the people who were involved with racing and preparing the Lolas during the period of 1963 to 1974 for their help. Everyone I contacted willingly and enthusiastically took time out from other activities to sit down and reminisce, either by phone or in person. Without exception, everyone felt this was an important and long overdue project. The people who cooperated with me during the interview process were Eric Broadley, Laurie Bray, Dan Gurney, George Follmer, Bruce Burness, John Cannon, A. J. Foyt, John Mecom, John Collins, Charlie Agapiou, David Piper, Roy Pierpoint, Mike Coombe, Frank Gardner, Tony Maggs, Bob Olthoff, Richard Attwood, John Surtees, Mario Andretti, Parnelli Jones, Sam Posey, Chris Craft, Hugh P. K. Dibley, Skip Hudson, Sid Taylor, Lothar Motschenbacher, Jerry Grant, Carroll Smith, Chuck Parsons, Ed Leslie, Augie Pabst, Brian Redman, David Hobbs, Bill Krause, Roger Penske, Dick Guldstrand, Scooter Patrick, and Bob Bondurant.

Ann Hale, information officer at Lola Cars, has been terrific; Jack Sears and John Fitzpatrick of the British Racing Drivers Club (BRDC) helped me contact many of the English drivers; and Peter Sutcliffe put me in touch with Ken Stewart who supplied me with all of the excellent and extremely rare photographs of the Lolas racing in South Africa. Kathy Ager, formerly of London Art Tech, has once again helped save me from disaster with her professionalism. Alexis Callier, Doug Nye, and the late Jean Jacques Frei contributed a number of rare and wonderful photographs from the European events. Chris Knapman of Collector Carbooks saved my life by helping me secure many of the rare racing programs that I used to identify the cars in the pictures of the English events. Janos Wimpffen supplied me with hard-to-find entry and result sheets from many of the continental races, and they helped me considerably with driver identification. To all of these people, a huge thank you for helping make me and this book look great. It couldn't have been done without you.

Clive and Shelia Stroud, Jack Sears, John and Diana Whitmore, Peter and Liza Sutcliffe, Alan and Sharon Mann, and John and Liz Atkins provided me with a place to stay during my research trips to England. To all of you, a huge thank-you for your wonderful hospitality.

Any facts used in this book came from official race records, race programs, Automobile Year, and Autosport. Yet even with the aid of these very reliable sources, discrepancies are not uncommon. Race numbers are often incorrect or omitted completely, numerous drivers' names are omitted or badly misspelled, race dates are often incorrect, and complete races are omitted, for whatever reason, in various reports. Half the fun of doing a book of this type is trying to sort it all out.

Again, to everyone who helped, thanks for making this book the best that it can be.

—Dave Friedman

◉ **Augie Pabst on the gas during practice at Sebring.**

"The Lola was really quick in practice. The track at Sebring was really made for the Lola because we could use all of the power that we had to our advantage. That car was a winner, and it was very fast." —Augie Pabst

CHAPTER

LOLA MK.6 ARRIVES 1963-1964

In 1958, a young, unknown quality surveyor named Eric Broadley began to produce a small, under-2.0-liter, club racer that he called the Lola Mk.1. His company, Lola Cars Ltd. of Bromley, Kent, produced the Mk.1 successfully until 1962, and it enjoyed great success in club races worldwide, especially in England and the United States. In 1960, Lola also produced a front-engine Formula Junior, and followed that up with a mid-engine Formula Junior from 1961 through 1963. Those Formula Juniors were very successful in Europe, but, for some reason, very few if any made it to the major North American races. Lola also built Formula Two cars and enjoyed considerable success with them.

In late 1961, Yeoman Credit and Bowmaker formed the Bowmaker-Yeoman racing organization with Reg Parnell as team manager and John Surtees and Roy Salvadori as drivers. This new team commissioned Broadley and Lola Cars Ltd. to design and build an F1 Lola for the team to race during the 1962 season. At the Dutch Grand Prix—the first Grand Prix of the season—Surtees shocked the establishment by taking the pole position in the Lola's first Grand Prix race. Unfortunately Surtees was put out of the race with suspension failure on the ninth lap, but Lola had made its entrance to big-time racing. Surtees had several top-five finishes during the 1962 season, including two outstanding second-place finishes at the British and German Grands Prix. Surtees finished fourth in the season's end world championship points. This was an outstanding effort for a first-year manufacturer, but at the end of the season, the two financial companies, Yeoman and Bowmaker, withdrew support from the project, and Surtees signed on with Ferrari. Reg Parnell continued to campaign the Lolas in 1963 with Chris Amon as the driver, but very few decent results were achieved during that season.

By the end of 1962, some people in Europe were beginning to take note of the number of American-engined cars appearing in international sports car racing. Eric Broadley was one of those people, and in late 1962, he began to design a car that would help change sports car and endurance racing forever. Eric Broadley remembers, "We built the Lola Mk.6 coupe because it seemed like a good thing to do at the time. By late 1962 a big American engine in the back of a small GT car was, to me, the logical way to go, and time has proven that we definitely made the right choice. We had to work like hell to get the prototype ready for the Racing Car Show in January 1963, and the car wasn't much more than a shell when we finally got it to the show and put it on the display stand."

When the 1963 Racing Car Show opened at the Olympia National Hall on January 25, the most anticipated car was nowhere to be seen. On Saturday January 26, after 52 sleepless hours of work by Eric Broadley and his small staff, the Lola Mk.6 GT coupe finally debuted on its stand at the Lola display. *Autosport* reported, "The extremely low-slung, attractive car should give a good account of itself in Prototype races this coming season. Powered by a 4.2- or a 4.7-liter Ford V-8 engine, the little coupe has an estimated top speed of 180 mph which makes it much faster than any of the Grand Prix cars competing this season." *Motorsport* exclaimed, "Eric Broadley has built a fantastic Lola coupe with a 4.7-liter Ford V-8 engine behind the seats and a Colotti gearbox behind the rear axle. The first of these incredible machines, in mock-up form, was seen at the B.R.S.C.C. Racing Car Show, and two of these cars have been entered for Le Mans, which should cause the French scrutineers to choke on their Gauloises. Previously Maserati held the crown for

◉ **Augie Pabst and his Lola (00) prepare for the start of the 25-lap Nassau Tourist Trophy. Next to Pabst sits the Grand Sport Corvettes of Jim Hall (65) and Dick Thompson (80). George Butler (49) Shelby Cobra and Gordon Butler (149) Corvette String Ray sit on the second row.**

building 'wild ones,' but if this Lola-Ford works, then the crown must surely pass to Broadley."

Eric Broadley picks up the story, "We never had any time to test the car before we ran it at Silverstone in May. We had problems with a wheel falling off at the Nürburgring, and we were rushing about trying to get a second car ready for Le Mans. That didn't happen, however, and I drove the one car that we had finished to Le Mans with a mechanic riding with me. When we finally got on the track after a terrible row with the French scrutineers, the car went bloody well until the gearbox packed it in and David Hobbs crashed. We were very happy with the overall concept of that car, and we were thrilled by the way that it ran. Looking back, it would have been nice to carry on with that project. Our intention was to develop the Mk.6 into a full-fledged racing car, but we would have had to raise considerable financing at that time, and I'm not sure how we could have done that. When Ford entered the picture in mid-1963, it was an answer to our financial problems and we went with it. Our choice was a bit of a pity really, because the Ford GT, as a race car, was a bit of a backward stab. That car was heavy and it was made of steel, but it became a good project; it solved some of our money problems, and it wasn't too bad to work on."

In 1963, team owner John Mecom managed to get his hands on one of the three Lola Mk.6 GTs, much to Ford Motor Company's consternation. Undoubtedly, Ford was even more upset when Mecom installed a Traco Chevrolet engine in the car that was intended to carry a Ford engine in its backside. Augie Pabst drove the Lola in its first two races at Nassau in December 1963, and he created a sensation by winning both races handily. After Nassau, however, the fortunes of the Mecom Lola GT changed, and nagging mechanical problems frequently prevented the car from finishing. In October 1964, while practicing for the Times Grand Prix at Riverside, Augie Pabst destroyed the car in a spectacular crash from which he was lucky to escape with his life. In the ensuing years, all three of the Lola Mk.6 GT cars have found a new life and happiness as restored and privately owned historic race vehicles.

◉◉ When the Racing Car Show opened at Olympia National Hall on January 25, 1963, the most widely anticipated display was nowhere to be found. It wasn't until the following day that the Lola Mk.6 GT coupe arrived on its stand in the Lola booth. To say that it created a huge amount of interest would be a gross understatement.

"I first saw the Lola GT at the Racing Car Show in January 1963, and I thought it was lovely. It was just marvelous, and I immediately decided that I wanted to drive it, which I eventually did. Eric was always fairly innovative, and that car was quite innovative with its fantastic looks and monocoque chassis. It was one of the first serious mid-engine cars.—David Hobbs

◉ As a last-minute replacement for John Surtees, Tony Maggs started the sports car support race at the May 1963 Silverstone International Daily Express Trophy from the back of the pack. Maggs put up a terrific drive in a completely unfamiliar car to finish ninth overall.

"I knew and liked Eric Broadley, and I had driven Lola F2 cars for the Midland Racing Partnership for a number of seasons. I had also driven Aston Martins and Ferraris in GT racing so I had considerable experience in that form of racing prior to May 1963. When I was asked to drive the Lola GT at Silverstone, I had never really seen the car before, much less sat in it. John Surtees was supposed to drive the car, but because John was then under contract to Ferrari and they put their foot down, he had to back out at the last moment. I was called up on the public address system about 20 minutes before the start of the race, and Eric and John asked if I could help them out. As a friend of John Surtees, I think that I just happened to be free at the right time to help them out of their difficulty. I had seen the Lola in the paddock that morning and I had admired it. I can recall being very impressed with the car's possibilities, although I think that they had just finished it at the last moment. I can't be certain, but I don't think that John had practiced the car the previous day [he had and turned a lap of 1.50.2], because the whole Lola GT thing was one of those products of much midnight oil. I think that at that time, the Lola was a totally new concept in both looks and design. Even by today's standards that Lola was a most beautiful car. The Lola was like nothing that I had ever driven before. That car had sufficient visibility, was extremely quiet inside with what one could almost call a 'boulevard' ride, and it was very forgiving and sure-footed. I can also remember that the brakes were rather spongy but very efficient and that the engine power was smooth but nothing startling. The car seemed to stick to the track like glue, but I never really had the opportunity to have a go because the race was too short. The Lola did tend to keep one rather occupied, and by the time I started to settle in, the race was over. As I remember, about every second corner had its interesting moments. The gearbox had very little feel to it, and you were never sure if you were in gear or not. The clutch was the only real problem, because Eric had fitted a clutch that was apparently designed to increase its bite at high revs on some sort of centrifugal system, or so I was told. What actually happened was that on braking into the corner with the power off, the clutch would completely disengage and the engine would stall. Having set the car up for the corner and now needing power to control it, you would go for the throttle only to find what felt like a big box of syrupy neutrals and a deathly hush from the rear. On the slower corners this wasn't so bad, but on the quick ones the 'drive with the right hand, feel for the starter button with the left' technique tends to place unusual pressure on the teeth and gums. It took me quite a few laps to realize that the car wasn't jumping out of gear as I first thought, and that to let go of the throttle completely made you an instant heart-failure candidate. Toward the end of the race, I realized that the secret was to brake and keep the revs up at the same time, boot the throttle before you needed it or wanted it, and hope that the clutch agreed as to when it should again apply drive to the rear wheels. Unfortunately, the event wasn't long enough for me to master this technique. All this did, however, show just how forgiving the car was. It must have been, as we did achieve some most unusual attitudes and, I think, raised a few eyebrows on some of the other competitors." —Tony Maggs

◉ Tony Maggs (in car) helps to set the rearview mirror as Rob Rushbrook (left) and Don Beresford (obscured by roof) make a last-minute check of the engine prior to the start of practice for the May 1963 Nürburgring 1,000 Km.

"After Silverstone I didn't think that there were any future plans involving myself with Lola, but when John could not drive the car, Eric asked me to drive it at the Nürburgring. I had competed at the Nürburgring in F1 grands prix and in the 1,000-kilometer events, and it was my favorite circuit. I remember feeling fairly strongly about the clutch and probably suggested that Eric use it as an anchor for his boat. There had been no instability evident at Silverstone, and I think that the lovely Lola kept it well tucked away in her wheel arches as a surprise for later on. Except for a new clutch and, I think, a bit more power from the engine, the car was the same at the Nürburgring as it was at Silverstone." —Tony Maggs

◉ The beautiful Lola coupe drew looks from curious spectators wherever it went. A very young Jochen Neerpasch (light-colored overcoat) is among the onlookers.

◉ Tony Maggs (left) and Eric Broadley (right) discuss driving conditions at the Nürburgring.

"Eric let me select my co-driver, and I chose a fellow South African, Bob Olthoff. Bob was an outstanding and upcoming young driver but had never enjoyed the break that he deserved. He also possessed extensive mechanical knowledge, knew the Nürburgring, and was always great fun to work with." —Tony Maggs

◉ The Lola GT sits in the pits during practice and qualifying. The car suffered from carburetor and gearbox problems during practice, and Maggs could only manage a lap of 10.00.01.

"I can't remember any real difficulties during practice except for the car's aerodynamic enthusiasm, some carburetor difficulties, and Bob's incident when the gearbox jammed in second gear just after the pits and he had to complete the whole 14 miles in that gear. When Bob didn't appear on time, Eric was convinced that he had lost it somewhere, and my suggestion of a co-driver wasn't very popular for a while." —Tony Maggs

"Eric Broadley was a bit nervous about me driving the car, and his nervousness reached an intense level when it took me 20 minutes to complete the scheduled eight-minute lap due to a transmission problem." —Bob Olthoff

◉ The Maggs/Olthoff Lola (115) got a good start at the 1963 1,000-km race.

"I very much enjoyed driving the Lola Mk.6 at the Nürburgring in 1963. That was my first drive in a V-8-powered car, and it was the most powerful car that I had driven. Before the Lola, I had been racing my twin-cam MG. That Lola was a very quick motor car even though it wasn't sorted out at that point. The car handled really well, but we had problems with the gearbox and problems with the wheels falling off. The drive gear breaking on the distributor is what finally put us out of the race. We were young and foolish in those days, and we didn't care that on the jump on the main straight, the car was landing on its front wheels with the back ones still in the air." —Bob Olthoff

◉ The Maggs/Olthoff Lola coupe heads down the hedge-lined straight at the Nürburgring early in the race.

"The Nürburgring allowed the Lola to produce her trump card. She would behave impeccably and was a joy to drive around the circuit until she saw those humps down that long, fast, hedge-lined straight. She would rush over the hump, joyfully kick her rear wheels in the air, and forget to put them back on the track on the way down. That's a 'Polish Wheelie' to the bike boys. It was necessary to come right off the throttle to prevent the revs from going off the clock and then wait patiently for her to get her act together before applying power. She could get quite nasty about it if you didn't allow her to enjoy herself and started applying the throttle too early. The final hump on the straight was followed immediately by a very fast left-hander. At this point, both Bob and I found her rather reluctant to turn left while running on the front wheels only. We did improve matters slightly by widening the hedge on the exit to the corner by the use of some judicious pruning during practice. If you cooperated with her on this section of the circuit, she would behave sweetly on the rest." —Tony Maggs

◉ The Maggs/Olthoff Lola was running a well-paced plan before trouble set in.

"During the race, the right rear wheel came off while I was driving. I can't for the life of me remember the name of the place, but it was the right-hander just before coming out of the woods about four corners before the main straight. [A study of an old track map shows this spot to be Brunnchen.] The wheel incident began with my hearing a musical tinkling noise accompanied by a feeling of being closely followed. The rearview mirror showed a well polished chrome knock-on wheel nut trying hard to overtake me. I remember thinking of this as being rather strange because no other competitor was in sight. A second or so later the right rear wheel came off the hub and with nary a twitch, lodged itself in the wheel arch, and we came to a gentle halt with the wheel nut in close attendance. The problems began when a careful search of the boot produced no tools or jack of any kind. Accepting outside assistance, material or physical, was grounds for immediate disqualification. This being a favored spectator area, offers of tools, jacks, hammers, alcoholic beverages, and advice in German [were plentiful]. A head-scratching tour along the inside fence revealed an approximately 15-foot-long fir sapling that had been cleaned and then discarded by someone. By inserting the tree under the chassis and the use of a convenient loose rock as a fulcrum, I could raise the rear of the car as long as I sat firmly on the far end of the sapling. The fact that I hadn't been gifted with 15-foot-long arms was only solved by a further time-wasting search for heavier-than-I-was rocks to replace myself as ballast. I refitted the wheel and broke the remaining stones in the area tightening the wheel nut. Back in the pits there were mutterings about left- and right-hand threads, a few solid clouts with a very large hammer, and Bob departed. I can't recall how many laps later it was, but Bob stopped about a mile beyond the pits with a sheared distributor drive. Bob was a fairly determined sort of fellow and, having determined that there was no chance of repairing the damage, decided that after the rather strange looks he had received following his second-gear lap during practice, he ought to let the pits know that the car was not a total write-off. The shortest way back seemed to be via the interior access roads. This meant climbing over the fence into the spectator area, an act that was, according to a local representative of the law, most strictly verboten. Having no success with Afrikaans, English, what sounded vaguely like French, or waving his driver's armband, and having been pulled off the fence by the law for the fourth or fifth time, Bob decided that a show of force was the only avenue left open to him. From the top of the fence he backhanded the by now extremely irate lawman in the face and clamored over the fence to be swallowed up by a supportive and cheering crowd. He claimed that the last view of his opponent, minus his cap and flat on his back in the grass, was the man desperately trying to draw his firearm. On Bob's arrival back at the pits, the whole team decided that a discreet withdrawal was the wisest move. So ended a rather unsuccessful outing." —Tony Maggs

◉ The Maggs/Olthoff Lola in the world famous Nürburgring Karussel during the 1,000-km race.

"I had no further contact with the car after Nürburgring. Besides getting a little carried away on the straight, the car handled very well and was a pleasure to drive. I believe that had one had the opportunity to really sort out the car, she would have been extremely quick. The Lola didn't have the snarling rough ride that was expected from a Ferrari, but seemed to float along with all four wheels —mostly that is —glued to the tar. It always remained very controllable and gave one a great sense of confidence. Even while playing her joyful young colt act down the main straight, one never felt that she was going to get away from you. It sort of left you with a feeling of mild surprise. I can't think of any other major problems besides her somewhat unusual behavior over the roller coaster main straight. On thinking back, I'm not at all sure that this was only aerodynamics. There was a lot more to it, including shock absorber rebound, weight distribution, and probably many other factors. I cannot remember the car showing unstable tendencies at any other time, including Silverstone, where fairly high speeds were reached. It is rather difficult to give a clear opinion of the car, as it was very much an untried and untested prototype. The original Lola was, in my opinion, the most beautiful car that I have ever seen. The later Ford GT developed all of the modern 'teeth and toenails,' fins, wings, spoilers, ducts, etc., and although no doubt a much faster car, it had, in my mind, lost much of its character. That first car could have won a beauty competition anywhere." —Tony Maggs

◉ Eric Broadley drove the Lola coupe to Le Mans. An unwelcome surprise in the form of technical rejection awaited the Lola team when they showed up for scrutineering.

"We set out to build two cars for the 1963 Le Mans race, but we only got one finished. We were in such a rush to get to the circuit that we decided to drive the coupe to Le Mans ourselves. The clutch that we had in that car was bloody awful, and it made the car pretty difficult to drive on the road. At that time there was an air ferry that went across the channel, and we drove the car down to the ferry in the early morning. When we got to the ferry the guys that worked there said, 'We'll have to drive it on the aircraft because you can't drive it on to the aircraft.' I said, 'You'll never drive this thing; the clutch is terrible.' He said, 'No problem, I'll get it up there.' This bloke hops in the car, puts it in gear, and drives it right in to the airplane, no problem at all. Well, I damn near hired him on the spot. When we got to France we drove onto Le Mans. The roads in France were pretty terrible then, and we got in a few slides along those roads. The front suspension was the rubber bushings that we used in those days, and we had to stop several times to tighten the bolts that held the wishbones in place. Our truck didn't travel with us because it had gone ahead earlier and crossed the channel by sea. We were lucky because Don Beresford and I carried some of our spanners with us in our pockets." —Eric Broadley

◉ Because the car was rejected by the French officials, numerous modifications had to be made to the rear deck, and valuable practice time was lost.

"In 1963 I was driving for Midland Racing Partnership [MRP] in a Formula Junior Lola. We were racing the factory Lola in the British Formula Junior Championship and also on the Continent. That was my first introduction to Lola and Eric Broadley. Richard Attwood, who was one of the partners in MRP, had co-driven with me in my Lotus Elite at the Nürburgring in 1962, and later that year he let me drive his Cooper Junior at Oulton Park. That was my first single-seater drive, and I won the race in the rain. When Eric built his prototype Mk.6 GT, he asked Dickie and me to drive it at Le Mans. That car was beautiful to drive; it was absolutely fantastic. The car was incredibly late getting to Le Mans. Dick and I were at the factory in Slough the week before Le Mans, and the car wasn't even close to being finished, so we jumped in my car and drove to Le Mans to get our licenses. Eric drove the coupe to Le Mans, and it didn't arrive until Wednesday, which was the first day of practice. We immediately ran into a huge snafu over the car's compliance with the French regulations. In those days, the scrutineering was done in a big field, and you took the car from tent to tent hoping that you would pass. You had the butcher, the baker, and the candlestick maker acting as scrutineers, and they knew as much about cars as my little finger. You never knew what they were going to do or going to say. It seems that the 'Magic Box' [a box that simulates a suitcase] wouldn't fit in the boot, and after some very heated words, changes were made, the car was finally passed, and we were allowed to practice." —David Hobbs

◉ Peter Jackson (right with glasses) and Eric Broadley (left by mirror) work frantically to complete the required Lola modifications, and the car passed before the allowed practice time ran out.

"Everyone was tremendously interested in seeing the car run, but we had a hell of a lot of problems just trying to get it through scrutineering. The airbox went in through the roof, and it gave no rear vision down the center of the car. The French organizers would not accept that. The mechanics had to flatten off the engine bay behind the driver and take the intakes out through the side of the car. Peter Jackson of Specialized Moldings and many others lent a hand to put the car right, and in the end the organizers were very helpful; but in the beginning they were absolute bastards because they made us change the whole bloody car. The organizers really wanted the car to run because it was such an interesting car. That car foresaw everything that was about to come in the immediate future." —Richard Attwood

"We had horrendous problems with the French scrutineers at Le Mans, and we ended up working night and day to put the car right so that they would let us run it. They wouldn't accept our original rear deck design, and we had to redesign the whole bloody thing on the spot."
—Eric Broadley

◉ The Lola coupe sits in its starting position awaiting the start of the 1963 Le Mans race. The car elicited a huge amount of interest among the spectators and the participating manufacturers.

◉ **The Attwood/Hobbs Lola coupe at speed in the early hours of the race.**

"When I drove the Lola Mk.6 at Le Mans in 1963, it was a very revolutionary car. That sort of rear-engine GT car had never been done before, and it was really exciting to be in on the ground floor of something so special. The worst part of the car was the bloody gearbox. The way that the gears were changed in that car gave us trouble from the start. I think that the gearbox itself was reliable, but because of the way that you had to change the gears, it was impossible for it to work in that car. That Lola was hugely quick considering the tires that we had then." —Richard Attwood

The Attwood/Hobbs Lola (6) leads the Salvadori/Richards Jaguar E-Type out of the Mulsanne Hairpin.

"In the race the car ran reasonably well, and we were up to eighth place when it all started to come apart. We had some engine problems and the gearbox broke, necessitating a long [two hours] pit stop. When I rejoined the race I only had two gears. I don't think that the gearbox was one of that car's strong points. Because the car was so new, there were a number of things that needed tidying up, and the Colotti gearbox was one of them. Even with just two gears, I managed to set one of the quickest lap times of the race, and the Lola was pretty damn fast on the Mulsanne Straight. The Lola's speed was on a par with all of the other competitors, and I don't remember anyone passing us on the straight."
—David Hobbs

Late in the afternoon, the Lola rushes through the esses. A few hours later, disaster would strike in this same area.

"About five in the morning, going into the esses, the gearbox got all jammed up and I misselected a gear and spun. The next thing I remember is hitting the left side bank in the esses and making a real mess of it. I was quite anxious to get out of the car because I knew that Willy Mairesse's Ferrari was not far behind, and as we all know, Mairesse was known as a bit of a crasher. I was terribly disappointed by what had happened, and I know that Eric was bitterly disappointed about the turn of events. Everyone involved with the Lola had put a huge effort into that car, and the final outcome was a tremendous disappointment to all of us. All in all, the Lola was a very good and a very beautiful car, but Eric never ran it again." —David Hobbs

◉ In his first drive in the Lola Mk.6 that John Mecom had just bought, Augie Pabst starts the 1963 Guards Trophy at Brands Hatch at the back of the pack due to lack of practice. At this race, contrary to popular belief, the Lola still had a Ford engine in it, not a Chevrolet. Pabst's race lasted four laps before the engine let go. In this photo Peter Sargent (19) Jaguar E-Type leads the field early in the race as Peter Sutcliffe (20) Jaguar E-Type, Maurice Charles (31) Jaguar D-Type, Innes Ireland (23) Aston Martin 214, Tommy Hitchcock (27) Ferrari GTO, Lucien Bianchi (3) Maserati Tipo 151, Lucky Casner (9) Maserati Tipo 61, R. C. Kerrison (29) Ferrari 250 GT Speciale, and Augie Pabst (3) Mecom Lola Mk.6 GT Ford give chase.

"I drove the Lola Mk.6 coupe for John Mecom, and it was an awesome car to drive when—and if—it ran properly. I joined the Mecom team in 1963 after I left Briggs Cunningham's operation. Roger Penske convinced me to join that team, and for some reason I was assigned to the Lola. I drove the Lola for the first time at the Guards Trophy in August 1963, and it still had a Ford engine in it. The car only lasted four laps before the engine blew. The car was very loose, and I was dirt tracking around every corner at Brands Hatch until we had the engine problem. I remember that Eric Broadley took me for a ride in the car on the street before I drove it at Brands. He scared the shit out of me because it was raining, and we were racing over some very narrow brick roads. Luckily we didn't hit anything, but you couldn't have convinced me of that at the time. That was one of the few times in my life when I was really scared." —Augie Pabst

◉ This is the only known photograph of the Lola test that was conducted by Ford at Monza in late October 1963. At this point in time, the Lola was the "test mule" for the soon-to-come Ford GT40, and Bruce McLaren was the test driver. Bruce's comment after the Monza test: "I think this car will be in the news next year."

"Lola didn't have the resources to project the Mk.6 onto the world stage, and that's why Eric went with Ford. That car was the forerunner of the GT40, and a lot of the GT40 ideas were tested on the Mk.6." —John Surtees

◉ John Mecom's Lola-Chevrolet sits in the Nassau garage surrounded by three Grand Sport Corvettes.

"At Nassau in 1963, I worked on the Lola coupe that Augie Pabst drove there. That was a great little car—very fast—and we had the Traco 327-cubic-inch aluminum Chevrolet engine in it there. Augie won a preliminary five-lap race and the Tourist Trophy in that car, and he raced it several other places in 1964." —Frank Lance

◉ Chevrolet came to Nassau loaded for bear, and as if by magic, many of the Chevrolet R & D engineers appeared to be having a Nassau vacation at the same time. Zora Arkus-Duntov (left) and crew chief Frank Lance (far right) work on the Lola's engine as John Mecom (foreground) looks away briefly.

"I was on my honeymoon in Europe when I read an article about the Lola Mk.6 coupe and became interested in possibly buying one. I stopped in London, met with Eric, and bought the car. I also think that it helped Eric out a bit financially too. Of the three cars, I got the only one that was ever raced by a private team, and of course, our car was raced many more times than the others. Augie did very well in that car, and he loved driving it; but we had continuous overheating problems that we were never able to solve, and he never was able to really show what we knew that car could do. Our getting that car caused a huge ruckus at Ford Motor Company. I was summoned to Ford for a big clandestine meeting that was so secret that we couldn't even meet at Ford, so we met somewhere near the airport. When I arrived at the appointed place, I walked into this big motel meeting room and sat down. One of the people who was in charge of the GT40 project, who will remain nameless, said, 'Goddamn it, when is that fucking Texan going to get here so we can fleece him and get this over with?' I said, 'Maybe, sir, you're talking about me. I'm here.' They tried everything in the world to buy that little car back from me and remove it from circulation. Needless to say, it didn't work. That was a beautiful little car, and it was one of my favorites." —John Mecom

Roger Penske (50) in a Corvette Grand Sport leads the field away for the start of the five-lap preliminary GT Race at Nassau in December 1963. Race winner Augie Pabst (00) Lola Mk.6, Dick Thompson (80) Corvette Grand Sport, Jim Hall (65) Corvette Grand Sport, John Everly (106) Cobra 289, Art Riley (51) Volvo, and Mike Gammino (23) Ferrari GTO follow Penske toward the first corner. This is the only race at Nassau in which all three of the Grand Sports competed.

Augie Pabst sits in the coupe talking to John Mecom (foreground) and his crew before the start of the Nassau Tourist Trophy.

As the green flag falls at the start of the Nassau Trophy Race, one of the Corvette Grand Sports takes an immediate lead over the rest of the field. Pabst's Lola (00) is at the far left.

◎ Augie Pabst is on the move as he passes under the bridge on the start-finish straight.

"We never tested that car; if we had, we would have won a bunch of races with it. If that car had ever been properly sorted out, it would have blown the doors off of everybody and everything. That car had gobs of power, it had beautiful aerodynamics, and it handled beautifully, but we just never got it sorted out." —Augie Pabst

◎ On his way to victory in the Nassau Tourist Trophy, Augie Pabst (00) pulls away from previous leaders Jim Hall (80) and Dick Thompson (65).

"In the Nassau Trophy Race, I laid back behind the Grand Sport Corvettes for a while because my engine was overheating. When the Lola became covered by oil from the Corvettes, I said 'Screw this' and motored by them to take the win. By the end of the race, there was so much oil on my windshield that I couldn't see, but I won it anyway. Regrettably, those two races at Nassau were the only races that I ever won in that car." —Augie Pabst

Augie Pabst in the winner's circle after completion of the 1963 Nassau Tourist Trophy.

When the Lola arrived at the Sebring technical inspection in March 1964, it did not suffer a repeat of the 1963 inspection disaster at Le Mans.

Frank Lance gives the engine a final check before practice begins.

"We had all kinds of problems with that car at Sebring. We had to do a lot of electrical work to hook up all of the lights, and the car had a mechanical tach." —Frank Lance

⬤ The Lola Mk.6 sits outside the hangar that the Mecom team used as a garage as Walt Hansgen (left) and Augie Pabst (right) enjoy a light moment.

⬤ Walt Hansgen (20) Lola-Chevrolet leads the Colgate/Baker Austin-Healey prototype out of the Webster Turns. The Lola started from 63rd because it had not recorded a qualifying time due to mechanical problems.

⬤ Shortly after the start of the race, problems descended upon the Lola. Under the watchful eyes of spectators, photographers, officials, and a Mecom team mechanic, Walt Hansgen (with hand in the engine compartment), attempts to re-time the engine well enough to be able to drive the car back to the pits. After repairs, the Hansgen/Pabst Lola-Chevrolet made a vain attempt to rejoin the race, but the engine blew on the 44th lap.

"Shortly after the start of the race, the tach cable seized, cranked the distributor around, and got everything out of time. One of our mechanics, and Walt, walked over to where the car was parked, and they timed the engine good enough to get back to the pits. The damage was done, however, and the engine broke shortly after the car re-entered the race." — Frank Lance

When the Lola showed up at Mosport for the Player's 200 in June 1964, the old engine gremlins still prevailed, and the car was parked before qualifying began.

"Once again, the motor let go in practice at the Player's 200, and I wound up driving the Shelby King Cobra that Dave MacDonald was supposed to drive before he was killed the week before at Indianapolis. I finished second overall in that car. God, if we would have only tested that Lola the way we would have tested that car today." — Augie Pabst

Augie Pabst (left) makes a point to John Mecom (right) at the Road America June Sprints in June 1964. Frank Lance is behind Mecom.

Sitting at the front of the grid waiting for the start of the June Sprints main event are Hap Sharp (65) Chaparral 2, Walt Hansgen (8) Lotus 19-Buick, Augie Pabst (2) Lola-Chevrolet, Charlie Gates (28) Genie-Chevrolet, Dick Doane (29) Chevette, and Roy Kumnick (41) Cooper-Cobra. The Lola led the race before succumbing to overheating problems.

◉ Augie Pabst watches Frank Lance (right) and other Mecom crew members add water to the Lola's overheating engine. Unfortunately, the leak cost the team the race.

◉ When the Mecom team went to England in August 1964 to compete in the Guards Trophy race at Brands Hatch, the Lola was one of the cars chosen for the trip. Augie Pabst (8) leads the John Coundley (36) Lotus 19 in a race for 11th place.

◉ The Mecom team returned to America and competed in the Road America 500 in September 1964. Augie Pabst (left) and Walt Hansgen (right) confer about the Lola's continued problems.

"After the Guards Trophy race, the car was flown from England to Milwaukee where I picked it up and drove it to my shop at Pabst Motors. We cleaned the Lola up, and I drove it up to Road America to make a few laps. The car wasn't geared for Road America, but we made a few test laps anyway." —Augie Pabst

◉ Draw your own conclusions regarding this sign seen at the 1964 Road America 500.

◉ Augie Pabst and Eric Broadley (dark shirt) confer about a problem that occurred after 30 laps of racing.

"At the Road America 500 in September, a problem occurred when the crew changed motors and someone forgot to install one of the engine mounts. The engine twisted over and popped the block out of the exhaust pipes so that it was lying on the gas tank."
—Augie Pabst

◉ The Lola sits in the paddock area at Riverside just before it was destroyed in a practice session for the 1964 Times Grand Prix.

◉ Final adjustments are made as practice is about to start. The double-wishbone independent rear suspension and Colotti four-speed transaxle unit are clearly visible here. Note the Ford Indy-type exhaust system mounted to the Chevrolet engine.

◉ The aftermath of Augie Pabst's Turn 6 accident at Riverside in 1964.

"My last race in the Lola was at the October 1964 Times Grand Prix at Riverside, and thank God that car had right-hand drive or I would have been decapitated. In the early practice sessions, I told the crew that the throttle was sticking. That night, Walt Hansgen and I went to the garage where the crew was working on the cars and we were both assured that the throttle problem would be checked out and fixed. Well, obviously, they never got around to it, because the next day the throttle stuck in the middle of Turn 6. I had a split second to think, do I put the clutch in and blow the engine or do I bounce the car off the guardrail? Before I knew it, I heard this horrible crash, and when I opened my eyes I said, 'Oh fuck,' because the guardrail had my head pinned against the rear window. My shoes had come off, my mouth was full of what I thought were teeth, the guardrail had skinned my wrist, and there was a strong smell of gasoline in the car. I thought, 'Well, I'm back in the hospital again.' When I spit my "teeth" out, I found out, happily, that it was only the glass from the windshield. That wreck was a shame because the Lola was such a beautiful car, and it was destroyed needlessly. Hell, that car had such tremendous potential, and if we had known then what we know now, John would have rented a track for testing and we would have won all of our races. That car was truly one of the best cars that I ever drove, and it gave me a hell of a lot of confidence. The biggest problem with the Lola was the overheating that we could never cure. Traco built our engines and they did a great job, but for some reason, we just couldn't get the damn thing to cool properly. If we could have cured the cooling problems, I'm sure that the engines would have stayed together and we would have won a lot of races." —Augie Pabst

CHAPTER 2

THE GLORY YEARS
1965-1967

By the end of 1964, American-engined cars were dominating big-time sports car racing in Europe and North America. The Jim Hall-built Chaparral was in its prime and was winning everything in sight in North America; the new Elva-McLaren was starting to show promise; Colin Chapman had built a Ford-powered Lotus 30 that was always a threat in the hands of the great Jim Clark; the Shelby King Cobra Cooper-Fords were still serious contenders in the hands of drivers such as Parnelli Jones, Richie Ginther, and Bob Bondurant; and the many one-off specials like Dan Gurney's Lotus 19B-Ford or A. J. Foyt's Mecom Scarab were always serious contenders any time they showed up at any racing circuit.

It was at this time that Eric Broadley began to see the possibilities that this type of racing offered, not only for competition and victories, but financially as well. Broadley remembers, "When we finished with the Ford project, we had some money in the bank and we were in pretty good shape. We decided that the Lola T70 would be our next step, and it was designed to be either an open or an enclosed car. The T70 was the car that really put us on the map, and drivers like John Surtees, David Hobbs, Hugh Dibley, Mark Donohue, and Dan Gurney drove the T70 to a number of wins in England and North America. Surtees really helped us in a big way by winning the Can-Am Series in America in 1966."

The racing debut of the T70 in the pouring rain at Silverstone was a success with John Surtees finishing second to Jim Clark's Lotus 30. Many teams and privateers on both sides of the Atlantic saw the potential of the car and placed their orders. John Mecom became the Lola distributor for North America, and his racing team—Walt Hansgen, Parnelli Jones, John Cannon, and Jackie Stewart driving—became one of the two teams that were capable of challenging and beating the all-conquering Chaparral 2 on the American circuits. John Surtees' team was the other. In England, John Surtees, Jackie Stewart, David Hobbs, Hugh P. K. Dibley, Paul Hawkins, Richard Attwood, and Roy Pierpoint proved that the Lola could beat the McLaren M1A and the Lotus 30 at Brands Hatch, Silverstone, Goodwood, and Oulton Park, as long as the engine lasted and none of the car's other frailties surfaced. Most of the engine problems that occurred in Europe were caused by the fact that the highly modified American engines would not run properly on low-octane European gasoline. Most of the problems that occurred in North America were caused by experimentation with new

⊙ **Brian Redman (33) Lola T70 finally got his chance to shine when he was offered a drive in the Red Rose Motors car. Redman finished fourth in the International Trophy Race.**

"I drove the Red Rose Lola T70 in 1966, and that was my first big car ride. The T70 was a big change from the lightweight E-Type Jaguar that I had driven previously. That Lola was so fast that there weren't any straights on the circuits anymore, and I had no time to relax because the next corner came up much faster than I was used to. I just wasn't used to so much power or so much tire on the road. We had a lot of grip and a huge amount of torque in that car. The first time that I raced that T70 was in the rain at Oulton Park. I came around Lodge Corner, which was a 90-degree right, then there was a dip and then a rise that you couldn't see over. It was sort of a straight, and in the past I'd always floored the Jaguar down that straight. When I floored it in the Lola, I instantly went backwards over Deer's Leap, right past the horrified eyes of the car owner who was standing on the pit straight. Once I got that car figured out, we had a very good year with it, considering that I was a novice. There were a lot of great people racing in those Group 7 races, and the competition was always tough, even in the club races. The Red Rose T70 was pretty competitive, very powerful, and it handled very well." —Brian Redman

engine technology such as fuel injection and carburetor setups, aluminum heads and blocks, and trick ignitions.

By the end of the 1965 season, the Lola T70 had established itself as the car to have if you wanted to be in the hunt. By the start of the 1966 season, almost every top driver was driving a Lola T70. Denis Hulme, Dan Gurney, Mark Donohue, George Follmer, A. J. Foyt, Jerry Grant, and Brian Redman were a few of the world-class drivers who joined the T70 ranks in 1966. Unfortunately, for the British fans, the Royal Auto Club (RAC) made the rather unpopular decision that Group 7 racing should be dropped in favor of F2 racing at the end of the 1966 season. This ludicrous call created a huge uproar among fans and competitors alike this type of racing had drawn record crowds to the various circuits since the "big bangers" started appearing in England in 1963. Denis Hulme and John Surtees dominated Group 7 racing in England, while John Surtees, Dan Gurney, and Mark Donohue won races during the inaugural Can-Am season. Surtees claimed the first Can-Am series championship by winning three of the six races, and the T70 won five out of six Can-Am races in 1966.

In 1967, the Lola 70 Mk.3 and Mk.3B appeared in both the roadster and coupe configuration. While the coupe was enthusiastically received, the roadster was not. The coupe, powered by an Aston Martin engine, was thought to be a serious British contender in the battle with Chaparral, Ford, and Porsche for the 1967 World Manufacturers Championship. That dream soon proved wishful thinking, however. The T70 roadster fared no better, proving to be too heavy and unmanageable to compete effectively with the new McLaren M6A, which completely dominated the Can-Am series that year. The only bright spots for Lola in the 1967 season were Mark Donohue's claiming of the United States Road Racing Championship (USRRC) Championship in the Sunoco Special and John Surtees winning the last Can-Am race of the year at Las Vegas in his year-old Mk.2.

The Lola coupe showed promise with the Aston Martin engine until a disastrous Le Mans. Chevrolet engines were installed in the coupes after Le Mans, improving performance but not reliability.

By the end of the year, it was painfully obvious that the roadster required some serious changes if it was to stay competitive in the North American marketplace. The coupe got a break, however, when the Federation Internationale de l'Automobile (FIA) decided to implement new endurance racing rules that would ban big-engine prototype cars from competing in 1968. The reason, as always, was too much speed and not enough safety. The FIA's new rules would breathe renewed life into the Lola T70 coupes.

⊙ Could Jack Brabham (far left) have possibly foreseen the success that the Lola T70 would enjoy between the years 1965 and 1967 when he first saw it at the Racing Car Show in January 1965?

◉ John Surtees conducted the initial tests on the Lola T70 at Silverstone under the watchful eye of Eric Broadley.

◉ The first race for the T70 was run under appalling conditions at Silverstone. The March 1965 Senior Service 200 saw Surtees finish second to Jim Clark's Lotus 30 after numerous spins and off-road excursions.

"John Surtees did a lot of the preliminary testing on the T70, and the car proved to be quite successful from the beginning. John had a very strong will, and I can remember racing early on at Silverstone in the rain. John was driving the T70, and we were racing against Jim Clark who was driving the Lotus 30. I kept telling John that we must put a spoiler on the car, but he wouldn't hear of it. It was a frightful day and we were the fastest car in the race, but John kept spinning off the course. He'd continue on, catch up to Clark, overtake him, and spin off again. After finishing second to Jimmy in that race, John came up to me and said, 'Enough of that, I think we ought to put a spoiler on the back of this car.'" —Eric Broadley

"Most of the success that I had in Group 7 and Can-Am racing was in a Lola T70, and that was because I was involved in the development and testing . . . from the very beginning. I was deeply involved with Ferrari during that time, and in October 1963, we brought one of the Ferrari sports racing prototypes to the Times Grand Prix at Riverside to test the waters, as they say. We found that for open-rules sports car racing, the Ferrari was far too heavy and also lacked the considerable horsepower that was needed to be competitive. I reported our findings back to Ferrari and told them that if they wanted to partake in that type of racing, they would have to build a more powerful engine and a much lighter chassis. In late 1964, Eric Broadley started to design and build the Lola T70, and about that time I decided that I wanted to broaden my horizons and keep up with the latest developments other than what was happening at Ferrari. Ferrari was rather isolated at that time, and I wanted to keep my fingers in what was happening with other developments in the outside world. I thought that this would help me tremendously in my feedback to the people at Ferrari. I asked Enzo Ferrari if he minded me testing and racing the Lola, and he said no because he saw the obvious advantage in having me do it. In early 1965, I tested the T70 and realized the potential of that car. We got the T70 sorted out, and, in 1965, I did some of the English and North American races with considerable success."
—John Surtees

Ⓐ Ⓑ Once people began to see the potential and the beauty of the T70, orders started to come into the Slough factory at a rapid rate. The monocoque chassis were constructed of sheet steel and light alloy, and the car bodies were laid-up by hand of partly stressed fiberglass. The first cars were available with a choice of Traco Oldsmobile, Traco Chevrolet, or Cobra Ford engines. The entire package weighed approximately 1,375 pounds, less fuel and driver. If you chose the Traco Oldsmobile engine, it would result in a savings of approximately 90 pounds.

◎ The first of the John Mecom Lola T70s appeared at the 12 Hours of Sebring in March 1965. When the green flag fell, John Cannon (22) was among the fastest of the strong field off the starting line. Cannon was the sixth fastest qualifier behind two Chaparrals, two Ford GT40s, and Dan Gurney's Lotus 19-Ford. Visible in this picture are Jim Hall (3) Chaparral 2, Ronnie Hissom (4) Chaparral 2, Ken Miles (11) Ford GT40, Richie Ginther (10) Ford GT40, Bob Grossman (26) Ferrari 330P, Pedro Rodriguez (30) Ferrari 330P, Ed Leslie (12) Daytona Cobra coupe, Bob Bondurant (15) Daytona Cobra Coupe, Ed Hugus (32) Ferrari 275P, Silvio Moser (8) Iso Rivota, and Delmo Johnson (1) Corvette Grand Sport. This was the Lola T70's first race in the United States.

"I drove the Ford-powered Lola T70 that John Mecom entered at Sebring in 1965. That was a very, very nice car to drive, and the car was just bloody gorgeous to look at. I was driving with a fellow named Jack Saunders. The night before the race I had dinner with Jo Bonnier and Mark Donohue. During our dinner, they both told me that I had a damn good chance in the race, but that I had to remember that the race was 12 hours long and not a sprint race. Even though the car was brand new, I knew that it was a damn good car, but we were hurting in the engine department because the Ford engine was mediocre at best." —John Cannon

◉ John Cannon (22) Lola T70 leads the first lap at Sebring. Following Cannon are Jim Hall (3) Chaparral 2, Ronnie Hissom (4) Chaparral 2, Dan Gurney (23) Lotus 19-Ford, Bob Bondurant (15) Daytona Cobra coupe, Pedro Rodriguez (30) Ferrari 275P, Ed Hugus (32) Ferrari 275P, and Delmo Johnson (1) Corvette Grand Sport.

"I was always very good at the Le Mans starts, and when the flag fell I got away well and led the first lap. I settled down to a steady pace, and I ignored all of the racing that was going on around me. The car was behaving quite well, and we were quite well placed. Jack took over after our first stop and promptly stuffed the car into something and broke the oil cooler. In actual fact, that problem probably didn't make any difference because the front bulkhead, where the steering rack attached, was quite weak and the attachment points for the steering arm were breaking away. If Jack hadn't stuffed it, we'd have been out of it anyway. I have very good memories of that car, and I drove it well within its capabilities compared to how I could have driven it. After the race, we had a debriefing with Eric Broadley at our shop in Houston. We discussed what the strong points of the car were and how to fix the weak points that showed up during the race. Walt Hansgen was the number one driver on the team, and he took over the Lola after the race at Sebring. I was absolutely enthralled with that car, and I couldn't wait for the second T70 to arrive because we were supposed to run a two-Lola team. On almost the same day that the second Lola arrived, Walt Hansgen wrote off the first one in a race at Mosport. That didn't leave much of a future for me at Mecom's, so I took off to California where I started driving for [actor] Dan Blocker." —John Cannon

◉ Although the Lola was withdrawn at 1:21 p.m. (less than three and a half hours into the race), work on the car continued into the night.

◉ At the Oulton Park Tourist Trophy in April 1965, David Hobbs suffered one of the most disappointing moments of his racing career. Hobbs (leading Jim Clark's Lotus 30) drove the Harold Young Lola T70 to a widely disputed second place behind the Brabham BT8 of Denny Hulme.

"In 1965, I drove the Harold Young Racing Ltd. Lola T70, and that car was awesome. We campaigned the car, in the beginning, with a 289-cubic-inch Ford engine, and that was a mistake because everyone else was using the Traco 355-cubic-inch Chevrolet engines. We were pretty successful for a small team, and we had our share of wins. The 1965 Tourist Trophy was one of the worst moments of my racing career. The TT was to be run in two two-hour heats. In the first heat we had a battery fire, which caused us to have an extra pit stop, and Denny Hulme, in the Sid Taylor Brabham BT8, beat me by a questionable two laps. The problem was that the checkered flag was thrown behind him and in front of me, so Denny got credit for an extra lap. In the second heat, I beat him by over a lap, but yet again, the flag fell between us and he got credited for yet another lap. In the end, my average speed and elapsed time were faster than his, but they gave the win to Denny. It was a complete fuck-up by the officials, and after hours of rather heated discussion with the RAC, they admitted that they had made a cock-up of the finish, but they wouldn't change the final results. That decision was absolutely devastating to the whole team —I mean it was absolutely devastating. Eric Broadley was crying, and I couldn't believe it. That would have been the first major, international win for the Lola T70, and it was stolen from us." —David Hobbs

◉ The start of the June 1965 Player's 200 at Mosport shows Hugh P. K. Dibley's (5) Lola T70 on the far left side of the front row. Also on the front row are Walt McKay (93) Cooper-Ford and Jim Hall (66) Chaparral 2. Though not visible in the photo, Bruce McLaren, John Surtees, and Jim Clark are in the group behind the front row.

"I was involved with the Lola T70 from the beginning because I had one of the first five T70s that were built. In 1965, I ran the Lola as a privateer after Tommy Atkins, who was going to run the car for me, committed suicide when he was diagnosed with cancer. After Tommy's unfortunate death, I was faced with having to maintain and organize the car myself, which is what I really wanted to do in the first place. I had a Traco Chevrolet engine in the car, and that engine wasn't too bad. I went over to the Player's 200 at Mosport where I should have come in second to John Surtees. I was motoring around quite slowly because the engine was overheating, and with a few laps to go I began to pick up the pace. I caught up to Charlie Hayes and overtook him for second place. I could see Surtees just ahead, but before I could catch him up, I got put off into a tree by a back marker in a Lotus 19. It was my own stupidity because the bloody idiot had not watched his mirror at all during the race, and I should have expected something stupid from him. After I got home, I repaired the car and raced it again in England. I pretty well coasted for the rest of the year." —Hugh P. K. Dibley

43

◉ John Surtees' (11) Lola T70 leads Jim Clark (82) Lotus 30 early in the race. Surtees won the race, and Mosport became the first major international win for the T70.

"In June 1965 I went off to do a race in North America where I won the Player's 200 at Mosport. This was the Lola's first major win, and it was a real turning point for us." —John Surtees

"Things got better for Lola in a hurry because John Surtees started winning in North America and I started to win in the UK. I won a race at Mallory Park on the same day that John won the Player's 200 at Mosport." —David Hobbs

◉ Walt Hansgen (16) gave his Mecom Lola T70 a good run at the August 1965 Guards Trophy to finish fourth overall in spite of suffering from a blocked fuel pipe. David Piper's (25) Ferrari 365P2 follows Hansgen's Lola through South Bank.

◉ John Surtees takes the checkered flag at the 1965 Guards Trophy. This victory was the first major win in Europe for the T70.

Walt Hansgen (left) and his protégé Mark Donohue sit in the Mecom Lola T70 that they were to co-drive at the September 1965 Road America 500.

The only car that could seriously threaten the Chaparral 2's winning ways in 1965 was the Lola T70. John Surtees and Walt Hansgen beat the Chaparral on several occasions when the Lolas could keep it all together. Walt Hansgen (11) and Jim Hall (66) stage one of their close, thrilling races at the Road America 500. Unfortunately, this exciting race was short-lived as the Lola went out of the race with mechanical problems and the Chaparral 2 cruised to victory.

◉ At the start of the Players Quebec race at St. Jovite in September 1965, John Surtees (2) Lola T70, David Piper (25) Ferrari 365P2, and Charlie Hayes (97) McLaren-Elva race to the first turn. Third-place finisher David Hobbs appears just behind Hayes' McLaren-Elva. Surtees won the race with Piper finishing second.

◉ John Surtees celebrates his second international victory in Canada within a three-month period.

> "I had a good go at St. Jovite, but I didn't know what awaited me at Mosport a week later. If I had, I would have gone home immediately." —John Surtees

◉ At Mosport, John Surtees confers with Jackie Stewart regarding a handling problem in Stewart's T70. This photograph was taken moments before Surtees was seriously injured in a spectacular crash that nearly took his life.

◉ When Surtees got into Stewart's car to check out a possible handling problem, disaster struck.

"A week after winning St. Jovite, I had a major shunt at the Canadian Sports Car Grand Prix at Mosport. I was driving a Team Surtees car when I crashed, but it was not my own car. We had two cars in Canada, and Jackie Stewart was my teammate for that race. Stewart was complaining about a handling problem with the car, so I took it out to see if I could sort out the problem. Jackie's car was the car that I had won the Guards Trophy with several weeks earlier, and, unfortunately, I lost a wheel on the fastest part of the circuit. The car hit a barrier, somersaulted over it, and landed on top of me. I also found out later that I was doused with petrol while trapped under the car. I remember nothing of the accident or the following four days except for what I have been told by others. Later on, we found out that the crash was due to the car being inadvertently fitted with an upright that had been badly cast in the states. That upright was somehow installed on the new car that I received just before the race at Brands Hatch. Unfortunately for me, the upright chose to break while I was driving the Lola at top speed. That was the most serious accident that I ever had, and it was pretty near the end of things for me." —John Surtees

◉ In October 1965, Walt Hansgen (17) Lola T70 and Hap Sharp (65) Chaparral 2 staged one of the most thrilling races ever seen at Laguna Seca. The two cars swapped places numerous times and were seldom more than a few feet apart.

◉ Walt Hansgen, running on seven cylinders, takes the checkered flag at Laguna Seca.

48

Hansgen receives the winner's trophy. This was the first major international win for the Mecom T70s.

"That race was a very exciting moment for me and for our team. Walt was running on seven cylinders, and he drove a hell of a race to hold off Hap's Chaparral." —John Mecom

Here is the type of line-up that made the Los Angeles Times Grand Prix for Sports Cars at Riverside one of the most anticipated events on the international racing calendar. Bruce McLaren (4) McLaren M1A and Jim Hall (66) Chaparral 2C sit on the front row of the over-2.0-liter qualifying race, while Parnelli Jones (18) Lola T70, Graham Hill (3) McLaren-Elva, Walt Hansgen (17) Lola T70, Jerry Grant (8) Lotus 19-Chevrolet, Hap Sharp (65) Chaparral 2, and Bob Bondurant (11) Lola T70 also await the start. McLaren won the race.

49

◉ Hugh P. K. Dibley (69) Lola T70 and Parnelli Jones (18) Lola T70 race for a top-five position early in the Grand Prix. Dibley finished seventh overall, while Jones dropped out of the race after 30 laps and running in fourth place.

"Toward the end of 1965 I came to Riverside to run in the Times Grand Prix. I ran a Lola T70 for SMART [Stirling Moss Auto Racing Team], and Friendly Chevrolet provided me with a good Traco Chevrolet engine. We ran well, stayed out of trouble, and finished seventh against some pretty incredible competition." —Hugh P. K. Dibley

◉ Bob Bondurant hits the Turn 6 wall on Lap 38 after leading the 1965 Times Grand Prix for 26 laps. Bondurant also recorded the fastest straightaway speed of the race at 163.63 miles per hour. It is interesting to note that even though he led the race for 26 laps, Bondurant's name appeared nowhere on the official final result sheets that were issued to the press by the raceway.

"The Lola T70 that I drove in 1965 was a beautiful car owned by Pacesetter Homes. Rick Muther had driven it at Laguna Seca, and he didn't get the job done, so John Krug, who was the owner of the car, asked me to drive it at the 1965 Times Grand Prix. That was a great car to drive, and it was really quick. I took the lead on lap 12, and I led the race for 26 laps before I hit the wall in Turn 6. The accident happened because I came into the corner a little bit too deep, and I locked the brakes up. That mistake was one of the most embarrassing moments of my racing career. I drove the car back to the pits for repairs, but trying to fix the damage turned into a total disaster and we parked the car for the rest of the race." —Bob Bondurant

◉ The David Good Lola T70 was shipped to South Africa for Roy Pierpoint and Doug Serrurier to drive in the October 1965 Rand Daily Mail 9-Hour Endurance Race at Kyalami. The Lola finished fourth overall.

"I drove my first Lola T70 at the 1965 Guards Trophy for a hillclimb chap named David Good. We used the Ford engine in our Lola, and in those days the Ford engines were not very reliable, so we didn't have the results that we should have had. This was the car that we took out to South Africa at the end of 1965 to run at the 9-Hour Race at Kyalami. My co-driver was Doug Serrurier, and we finished fourth overall. That Lola was really a lovely car and a great car to drive." —Roy Pierpoint

◉ After Walt Hansgen crashed his primary T70 at Las Vegas, the crew pulled out the spare car that Graham Hill had driven at the Times Grand Prix for Team Surtees and installed the engine from the wrecked Hansgen car. Frank Lance (kneeling at left) and the crew rush to complete the engine installation under the watchful eye of famed Indianapolis crew chief George Bignotti (far left).

"After Walt crashed our T70 in Las Vegas in 1965, we spent all day Saturday putting the engine from Walt's wrecked car into the factory car that Graham Hill had run at Riverside. Mecom had bought the car from Team Surtees after the Riverside race. In my opinion, those Lolas were really good cars, and they were very easy to work on."
—Frank Lance

◉ When the green flag fell on the Stardust Grand Prix, Parnelli Jones (18) Lola T70 took an immediate lead over Jerry Grant (8) Lotus 19-Chevrolet, Charlie Hayes (97) McLaren-Elva, and Chuck Parsons (10) Genie-Chevrolet and the rest of the field. Jones broke the gearbox on the 11th lap while leading the race, and Hap Sharp won in his Chaparral 2.

◉ Bob Bondurant (111) Lola T70 leads A. J. Foyt (2) Lotus 40 and the rest of the pack in the Nassau Trophy Race. Bondurant finished eighth in this race, but he did not finish the Nassau Governor's Trophy Race.

"I drove the T70 at Nassau, and I led the Governor's Trophy Race until a back marker put me in the weeds while I was lapping him. I did finish eighth in the Nassau Trophy race. That Pacesetter Lola was the best looking T70 that I ever saw. That car handled really well, and it was just a beautiful car to drive and to look at." —Bob Bondurant

◉ At the Las Vegas USRRC race in April 1966, well-known West Coast driver Bill Krause came out of a two-year retirement to drive the Pacesetter Lola T70.

"I drove the Pacesetter Lola in two USRRC races (Riverside and Las Vegas) in 1966. That car was very fast, but it was so different from anything that I had ever driven that I never felt comfortable driving it. I had been retired for about two years, and the Pacesetter people spotted me walking through the pits in Phoenix and offered me the ride. The Lola had a lot of weight in the back, and it was a bigger car than I was used to driving. You just couldn't throw the car around like I was used to. I could go fast down the straight and in the fast corners, but for me the Lola wasn't fun to drive through the slow corners because if you got the tail out you were in trouble. To me, the Lola wasn't a driver's car, and I didn't drive it long enough to really learn how to drive it properly. I ran pretty good in that car, but the Lola really needed someone who was more familiar with that type of car to drive it the way that it should have been driven. I was never comfortable in the car, and I think that I blamed a lot of things on the car that were really me. I felt that the car drove me rather than me driving the car. [It] was a beautiful and a well-prepared car, but it just didn't suit my driving style." —Bill Krause

◉ When the field was set for the April 1966 Tourist Trophy at Oulton Park, Denny Hulme (4) was the man to beat in the Sid Taylor Lola T70. Also in the field were drivers like Jack Brabham (2) Repco Brabham, John Coundley (26) McLaren-Elva, Brian Redman (28) Lola T70, Hugh P. K. Dibley (6) Lola T70, David Piper (38) Ferrari 365P2, and Frank Gardner (8) McLaren-Elva. Hulme won the race.

"I used to be a little private racer myself, and when a company called Team Elite went bankrupt, I bought a 2.0-liter Brabham BT8, and Denny Hulme drove that car for me. Denny won the 1965 Tourist Trophy race for our team in that BT8. We beat David Hobbs and all of those other guys who were driving the bigger Lolas, McLarens, Ferraris, and Cobras. In 1966, I got involved with running the factory Lola cars, and Denny Hulme won the Tourist Trophy race twice [1966 and 1967], along with numerous other races for us, in the T70 roadster. My recollections of that era are very simply put: great cars, great people, great racing, and great memories." —Sid Taylor

One of the Gurney-Weslake 305-cubic-inch Ford engines is readied at the All American Racers shop in Santa Ana, California, for installation in one of the team Lola T70s.

"Our small-block Ford engines were excellent. We didn't have the horsepower that the Chevys had, but we could rev them higher. With those Weslake heads, they were good, good engines." —Jerry Grant

An all-star line-up of sports cars appeared at Silverstone for the International Trophy Race in May 1966. Among the outstanding entries that lined up on the grid were Denny Hulme (32) Lola T70, Bruce McLaren (28) McLaren M1B, Chris Amon (29) McLaren M1B, John Coundley (14) McLaren-Elva, Hugh P. K. Dibley (22) Lola T70, and Brian Redman (33) Lola T70. Hulme won the race.

A large field of interesting cars, headed by polesitter Jerry Grant (8) Lola T70, arrived at Watkins Glen for the June 1966 USRRC race. Preparing to take the green flag are Mark Donohue (6) Lola T70, John "Buck" Fulp (26) Lola T70, Mike Goth (96) McLaren M1A, John Cannon (62) Genie-Chevrolet, Chuck Parsons (0) Genie-Chevrolet, Bob Bucher (29) Lola T70, Ed Hamill (65) Hamill SR-3, Mak Kronn (77) McKee SR-Chevrolet, and Bill Eve (52) Genie Mk.10-Ford. Fulp was the race winner.

Jerry Grant enjoys a drink of water while leading the early laps of the Watkins Glen race. Grant went out of the race with mechanical problems.

"I drove the Bardahl Lola for All American Racers in 1966. That Lola was a great car, and there was only one car that I ever liked better. That was the Lotus 19 that we had put a Chevrolet engine in and run for Allen Green Chevrolet in 1965. The Lola was a little harder to get adjusted to, but once you got it right it was really great. In the USRRC races, we sat on the pole about 90 percent of the time, and we also led most of the races that we ran. Our biggest problem was that we would break the ring and pinion because we were having heat treating problems with the rear end. That problem cost us a lot of well-placed finishes, but I did manage to win at Bridgehampton in 1966. That Bardahl car was the right combination of a great chassis and a damn good, light engine. That car was very competitive, and it was a comfortable car to drive for a big guy like me. I don't get comfortable in race cars very often. I should have been a football player, not a racing driver. Any car that Dan could drive I could drive, I just had to take the upholstery out of the seat. Without a doubt, those Lolas were better than the McLarens at that time. The McLaren was being changed so often that if you weren't in the pipeline, you didn't know what was going on. The Lola was almost like a spec racer, everything was standard and you always knew what you were going to get." —Jerry Grant

Mark Donohue had a spectacular, fiery crash in the Sunoco Lola at Watkins Glen. Penske Racing chief mechanic Karl Kainhofer (foreground) inspects what's left of the cremated Lola. Amazingly, Donohue walked away from the crash.

On August 7, 1966, Mark Donohue won the Kent, Washington, USRRC and gave Penske Racing its first major win. Who could have imagined at that time what Penske Racing would become in the future years? Karl Kainhofer carries the checkered flag on the victory lap.

Skip Hudson (9) Lola T70 leads Buck Fulp (26) Lola T70 at the Road America 500 in September 1966. Almost everyone who saw the Lancer Lola that Hudson drove felt that it was one of the most beautiful cars ever seen on a race track.

"We had a guy by the name of McQueen—not Steve—who was based in Laguna Beach, build the tail section for that Lola. We didn't have much money, and we were always down 25 to 50 horsepower because of it. We had a Traco Chevrolet engine, but we never had the finances to be able to buy the latest parts. Max Balchowsky worked on our engine and did a good job with what he had, but we just couldn't afford to get the parts that Max needed to make the engine competitive. We had two engines on hold at Traco, but we couldn't pay for them, and they ultimately went to John Surtees, who won the 1966 Can-Am Championship with them. When the team broke up, I wound up with the car. I didn't have the money to do anything with it, so the T70 sat around for quite a while. I loaned the car to a movie company for some filming at Riverside, and while on loan to that movie company, the Lola was flipped in the esses, destroying everything but the engine and transmission. After I got the wrecked car back, all of the usable parts were removed and we buried the car in a landfill in Rubidoux, California. The Lancer Lola now resides under a large apartment complex." —Skip Hudson

◉ The first Can-Am race was run at St. Jovite, Canada, in September 1966. When practice began, Paul Hawkins and Hugh P. K. Dibley were involved in spectacular crashes with their Lola T70s. Dibley's wrecked car is shown.

"I was involved with the T70 almost from the beginning, and I enjoyed driving those cars except when I did my flying act at St. Jovite in 1966. I arrived at the circuit after Paul Hawkins got airborne over the top of the hill and slid down the center of the road in an inverted manner. When I saw Paul after his crash, I told him that he shouldn't try to fly without a proper flying license, not knowing that soon I would make a real mess of it myself. I was aware that the car could get airborne, so I warmed up to my competitive speed gradually. I could feel the car go light and the revs climb as I went over the hill, but in the end I thought that everything seemed to be okay. I then decided that I would take the crest of the hill flat out. I was flat out in fourth gear and when I cleared the crest of hill, I could see the Quebec countryside and all of the beautiful fall colors. On lap 13 of practice, instead of seeing the beautiful countryside I saw blue sky and beautiful cumulus clouds, and I knew instantly that something was dreadfully wrong. I thought, 'Oh shit, this isn't quite right.' There was nothing for me to do but curl up in the left hand seat and wait until the accident finished. Because the Yank rules required it, this was the first time that I had ever used a lap strap, and that allowed me to curl up in the left-hand seat. The car cartwheeled through the countryside, and I thought, 'Shit, when is this damn thing going to stop?' When the car stopped, it was propped up so I just crawled out from underneath. Masten Gregory saw the accident, and he thought that I was a goner. When he saw me crawl out of the wreck, he thought that it was a ghost." —Hugh P. K. Dibley

◉ Two of the Lola T70's most prominent drivers, Dan Gurney (30) and John Surtees (3) in the 1966 Can-Am series, wait for practice to begin at San Jovite.

"When I departed Ferrari in 1966 after a serious argument, I came back to sports car racing with a new Lola T70 Mk.2. We won the first Can-Am championship with that car, and we also had some very good outings on the English circuits, winning the Guards Trophy again among others. We just used the standard package in that car, nothing fancy. Our major opposition in the Can-Am series that year came from the other people who had Lolas, like Dan Gurney and Mark Donohue, the McLarens of Bruce McLaren and Chris Amon, and, of course, the Chaparrals of Jim Hall and Phil Hill. Those damn Chaparrals were brilliantly engineered, and they were extremely quick with their powerful, aluminum Chevrolet engines. We used the straightforward Traco 5.0-liter Chevrolet engine. At that stage of the game, you didn't have a large works involvement with the series. You had car manufacturers like Lola and McLaren supplying many of the competitors with cars, but at that time, you didn't have the wholesale involvement of Ford and Chevrolet in providing special engines. Jim Hall was the one major exception, and Dan Gurney was doing some evaluation work for Ford, but that was it." —John Surtees

◎ Parnelli Jones (center) awaits the start of practice at St. Jovite. Jones' Mecom Lola was powered by a supercharged Ford engine.

"I got involved with the Lola T70 because I liked Eric and it seemed like a project that I would enjoy getting involved in. I set up the Lola distributorship here in 1965, and John Kalb, my team manager, was the one who actually handled that operation for me. The T70 was a really neat car, and at that time, it was the best of the bunch. We sold a lot of Lolas, and they were really beautiful cars to look at and to run. We had a lot of success with those cars, but we didn't do as much R&D as we should have. We lost a lot of engines, especially when we were experimenting with the supercharged Fords. That was a project that Lee Iacocca got me involved in, and it was a project from hell. That experiment was a very expensive undertaking that Ford never reimbursed me for. Parnelli was one of my favorite people, and he still is. No one could ever accuse him of not standing on the gas, because that's exactly what he knew how to do. He occasionally offended some of the Europeans with his bumping techniques, but that's racing, and he won races." —John Mecom

◎ John Surtees (3) Lola T70 and Bruce McLaren (4) McLaren M1B race for the lead at St. Jovite. These two great drivers finished in this order.

59

John Surtees was the winner of the first Can-Am race at St. Jovite on September 11, 1966. Surtees started on the pole and finished the race 6.5 seconds ahead of Bruce McLaren, setting a new track record for the race.

◉ When the Can-Am moved to Bridgehampton for the second round of the series, Dan Gurney (30) Lola T70 won the race. Behind Gurney are Chris Amon (5) McLaren M1B and Bruce McLaren (4) McLaren M1B, who finished second and third in the race, respectively.

◉ Dan Gurney becomes the first American to win a Can-Am race.

"The Lola T70 was a very good car, and I had the honor of being the first American to win a Can-Am race at Bridgehampton in September 1966. We won that race using our Weslake heads on one of our Ford 305-cubic-inch engines. The Lola T70 never appeared to be going particularly quick, but when you looked, the lap times were always there." —Dan Gurney

⊙ The John Surtees Lola T70 at the September 1966 Mosport Can-Am race. The lines of the beautiful Lola T70 are evident in this top-view photograph. Much of the aluminum used in the chassis, and the Traco Chevrolet engine with its cross-ram manifold and 58-mm Weber side-draft carburetors, is, seen here. Surtees stands in the cockpit.

⊙ Jerry Grant makes a rather serious off-course excursion in the Bardahl Lola during qualifying for the Mosport Can-Am. Grant did not start the race.

◉ Mark Donohue (6) Lola T70 leads Jim Hall (66) Chaparral 2E, and Phil Hill (65) Chaparral 2E early in the Mosport Can-Am. Donohue won the race, and Hill finished second. Jim Hall did not finish.

◉ Mosport was the first Can-Am win for Donohue and for Penske Racing.

"The Lola T70 was a very important part of the early years of Penske Racing. We won our first major races in 1966 with the T70, and without that car and the Sunoco sponsorship, I'm not sure that there would be a Penske Racing today." —Roger Penske

⊙ The crew of the AAR Lola prepares for the October 1966 Laguna Seca Can-Am. Watching from the background are chief mechanic Bill Fowler (left) and owner/driver (right) Dan Gurney.

⊙ Mechanic Malcolm Mallone at work on John Surtees' Lola during a break in the action at Laguna Seca in October 1966.

⊙ Jackie Stewart drifts his Mecom Lola out of Turn 9 at Laguna Seca. Stewart's supercharged Ford engine blew up in qualifying, and he did not start the race. Note the offset position of the supercharged Ford engine.

◉ Dan Gurney (30) Lola T70 and Chris Amon (5) McLaren M1B were front-runners in the early part of the Laguna Seca Can-Am, but both retired from the race with mechanical problems.

◉ Parnelli Jones (98) Lola T70 is on the move at Laguna Seca as he distances himself from Mark Donohue (61) and George Follmer (16), both in T70s.

"The Lola T70 was a really great sports car for its time. The T70 was very solidly built, but it lacked a wing like Hall was using on his Chaparrals. If that car had had a wing on it when I was driving it, it would have been even more dominant than it was. The car was pretty damn good in the first place, but it could have been much better with the wing. At Laguna Seca in 1966, we blew up our Ford engine in practice, and we switched to a Chevrolet engine before the start of the race. I could not properly qualify because of the engine change, so I had to start at the back of the consolation race in order to get in the main race. I won that consolation race. The race was run in two heats of 100 miles each with a break between the two heats. We had to start at the back of the pack in the first heat, and we wore a hole in the oil pan because the Chevy was a little bigger engine than the Ford. We came in and fixed that problem and went out and won the second heat after starting in the rear of the pack once again. I remember that John Surtees was running third when I caught him, and he was trying to keep me from getting by. Surtees was keeping me from catching the two Chaparrals, so I laid back until he wasn't so defensive. When he left an opening, I went under him and took out after the Chaparrals. I rubbed sides with him, and he spun off the track. John got a bit pissed off at me, but that's racing. John was a damn good racer, but he just didn't know the American way of getting by." —Parnelli Jones

◉ Denny Hulme (8) Lola T70 leads Skip Scott (91) McLaren M1A, George Follmer (16) Lola T70, and Chris Amon (5) McLaren M1B up the hill into Riverside's Turn 7. Hulme was driving the same Sid Taylor Lola in which he had scored so many early-season wins in England.

"We went to America to race in the Can-Am in 1966 and found ourselves up against some pretty tough competition. That was a pretty good era with some pretty great racers. It was absolutely a pleasure to run those cars during that time." —Sid Taylor

"The only reason that people like Denny Hulme, who was driving for Sid Taylor, and Hugh Dibley, who was driving for Stirling Moss' team, were able to get to America was because of the small amount of start money—in addition to the prize, contingency, and year-end money—that was being offered at the time. The [SCCA] decision to stop paying the start money was a very bad one because it ran off many good independent teams." —John Surtees

◉ Without a doubt, A. J. Foyt (83) and Parnelli Jones (98) are two of the most famous names in American racing. These two drivers were capable of driving and winning in anything that had wheels on it. Unfortunately for the fans, Jones and Foyt both retired early at Riverside due to overheating.

"That Lola was a fun car to drive and a good car to drive. The only problem with that car was that we never had time to sort out the big-block (Ford 427-cubic-inch) engine that Ford had us using. We had just gotten our car before the 1966 Riverside race, and we had very little time to do any work on it. We only ran the Lola at Riverside and Nassau because we didn't have any time for the other races. I enjoyed sports car racin', but our other racing commitments just didn't allow us to run any more of the Can-Am series. I would have loved to have run more of those races because those guys were real good racers. We raced everything that had wheels on it in them days—midgets, sprinters, championship cars, stockers, and sports cars. If it ran, we raced it, and that's why them days and them guys were so special."
—A. J. Foyt

◉ Mark Donohue (6) Lola T70, Chris Amon (5) McLaren M1B, and Mike Goth (86) McLaren M1B race for position at the 1966 Riverside Cam-Am race. Donohue finished fourth, Goth finished 10th, and Amon dropped out.

◉ John Surtees and mechanic Malcolm Mallone (right) celebrate their win at the 1966 Times Grand Prix.

After winning the Las Vegas Can-Am in November 1966, John Surtees is presented with the Johnson Wax trophy by Stirling Moss (left) and Johnson Wax President Samuel C. Johnson (right). This trophy was awarded to the Can-Am champion after the final race of the season.

"The Can-Am was a great series, and it could have been even greater if it hadn't gotten off track. I think the organizers should have been willing to help the teams with some financial assistance rather than putting all of the money in the prize fund. It is hard enough for an American team to exist on just its winnings, let alone a European team that has to mount a considerable effort just to get their cars and drivers to North America. This is why so many good efforts for that series were lost; it was just too bloody expensive to mount a serious effort, lasting several months, thousands of miles away from your home base. When we came to America in 1966, we operated on a shoestring. We had a Chevy truck, trailer, one car, and a maximum of three engines, but normally two engines. I had one mechanic and any local lads that wanted to help. I was the driver, mechanic, engineer, truck driver, and go-fer. We had nothing like the setup that Hall or Gurney had, but we won the championship anyway." —John Surtees

◎ Mario Andretti drove this Lola T70 at Nassau in December 1966 and didn't finish the Nassau Trophy Race, the only race that he drove during the 1966 Bahamas Speed Weeks.

"In 1966, I drove the Kar Kraft Lola that was equipped with a 427-cubic-inch Ford engine and a semi-automatic transmission. Kar Kraft was trying to come up with something that could compete with the Chaparral, but they were not capable of doing that. They were so far off in their efforts because they had absolutely no idea what the hell they were doing. That car was money wasted, and it was a real piece of shit. At Nassau, I was using a parking lot as a skid pad, and the car got away from me. I wound up in the bushes and damaged the nose, which couldn't be replaced for the race because we didn't have a spare." — Mario Andretti

◎ The start of the Nassau Trophy Race has Mark Donohue (7) Lola T70 leading Hap Sharp (65) Chaparral 2E, Skip Scott (91) McLaren M1A, A. J. Foyt (83) Lola T70, Buck Fulp (26) Lola T70, Peter Revson (92) McLaren M1A, and Sam Posey (82) McLaren-Elva.

Mark Donohue was the winner of the last Nassau Trophy Race in December 1966. The Bahamas Speed Weeks, ceased to exist after this race. Note the Pepsi Cola sponsorship on the side of the Penske Sunoco Lola.

The Lola T70 Mk.3 GT makes its debut at the Racing Car Show in January 1967. *Autosport* predicted that "with its low weight (1,700 pounds), the Lola will most certainly be a Group 4 winner as soon as it is homologated." The prediction was a little optimistic.

This "coupe," looking more like a T70 roadster with a partial top, appears at Sebring in March 1967. John "Buck" Fulp and USAC star driver Roger McCluskey were to drive the car in the race, but suspension damage caused the T70 to be withdrawn.

◉ John Surtees tests the Lola-Aston Martin at Goodwood in early 1967.

"The Lola-Aston Martin project was to be a totally British venture into the world of prototype endurance racing in 1967. The Aston-supplied engines showed some real promise in the early tests at Goodwood since we were able to run for 10 hours straight with no problems." —John Surtees

◉ John Surtees rounds the Mulsanne hairpin during the April 1967 Le Mans test weekend.

"We put up the fastest times consistently in the wet at the Le Mans test weekend, and we also were among the fastest cars in the dry. In fact, I remember that we were in the top three [third fastest] or four fastest cars at Le Mans for that entire test weekend." —John Surtees

◉ As the USRRC season opens at Las Vegas in April 1967, a full field of cars heads through the desert. Polesitter George Follmer (16) Lola T70, Mark Donohue (6) Lola T70, Skip Scott (91) McLaren M1A, Peter Revson (52) McLaren M1A, and Chuck Parsons (10) McLaren M1A are in a drag race to the first corner.

"It took awhile to get the car that I owned working correctly in 1967. That car was very fast, but we didn't have very good engine reliability. We were always short of money with the effort. Those Lolas were very good cars, and they had very good balance. You could go fast in them and be comfortable doing it." —George Follmer

◉ Bruce Burness (left) was, and still is, one of the most gifted mechanic/fabricators in racing. He and Trevor Harris were responsible for the extremely fast and well-prepared Lola T70 Mk.2 that George Follmer drove in the 1967 USRRC series.

"George Follmer had been driving a T70 for John Mecom in the 1966 Can-Am, and at that time Mecom was running supercharged Ford engines that were blowing up as fast as his people could build them. Mecom had to cancel out on Follmer because of the unexpected engine problems, and since he was the Lola importer, he sold his last new Mk.2 to George. Follmer approached myself and Trevor Harris to work on his car for the 1967 USRRC season, and we accepted. We took the car apart, went all through it, and installed one of the first Bartz Chevrolet engines that was ever built. After working on a McLaren, it seemed like so many of the small details were better on the Lola. There was no comparison between the two makes. The T70 was, in my opinion, the last of the really pretty cars. That car was a real trendsetter, and it was very user-friendly. [It] was also the first monocoque car that was readily available to everyone who could afford to buy one. The only drawback to that car, from my point of view, was that it was hard to work on. Follmer's car was very quick, faster than most, but we couldn't finish a race because Bartz was developing a new drive pump and the engine kept blowing up. George was relying on the prize money to keep the effort going, but when we didn't finish any races, Follmer ran out of money and the car was parked. We knew how to make the car go fast, but we didn't know how to race, and there is a big difference between the two. Penske's team knew how to race, and that's why they always won. We never thought about race strategy, we just hauled ass, and that's why, after a few laps, we were parked. That car was incredible, and George drove the shit out of it." —Bruce Burness

◉ At the 1967 Riverside USRRC, George Follmer (16) Lola T70 is, once again, on the pole with Mark Donohue (6) Lola T70 next to him. Peter Revson (52) McLaren M1A, Lothar Motschenbacher (11) McLaren M1A, Bob Bondurant (51) McLaren M1A, Bud Morley (71) McLaren M1A, Skip Scott (91) McLaren M1A, Jerry Grant (78) Lola T70, and Mike Goth (4) Lola T70 line up behind the front row.

George Follmer shows the effects of another blown engine.

Jerry Grant (78) Lola T70 leads Mike Goth (4) Lola T70 into Riverside's Turn 7. Grant did not finish the race; Goth finished fifth overall.

"I drove a Lola T70 for Allen Green Chevrolet in 1967, and of course, we had a big-block Chevrolet engine in that car. When the car ran, I had a tremendous amount of power at my disposal, but we had continuous engine development problems. We were using Hilborn fuel injection, and unlike Jim Hall, we hadn't been able to cure the problem of boiling the fuel. That particular T70 never achieved anywhere near its maximum potential. I led a lot of races with that Lola, but we never finished any. That car broke on me all the time, and it was not a good venture." —Jerry Grant

In May 1967, the USRRC made a stop at the beautiful Laguna Seca Raceway. Once again, George Follmer (16) Lola T70 and Mark Donohue (6) Lola T70 lead the field toward the very fast Turn 2. Lothar Motschenbacher (11) won the race in his McLaren.

Racing doesn't get any closer than this as Charlie Kolb (21) Lola T70, Peter Revson (52) McLaren M1A, and Skip Scott (91) McLaren M1A race through the very fast Turn 2 at Laguna Seca.

◉ At the May 1967 1,000 km of Spa Francorchamps, the Hawkins/Epstein (2) Lola-Chevrolet blows by the Spence/Hill Chaparral 2F and sets out after the Jacky Ickx–driven Gulf Mirage. It was obvious from the start that the Lola was in its element at Spa, and Paul Hawkins gave the coupe the race of his life. The Lola finished fourth overall and demonstrated why 1967 was such a spectacular year in international endurance racing.

◉ At the Targa Florio, the Epstein/Dibley Lola T70 coupe was not a major threat to the front-runners and suffered from numerous mechanical problems. The car lost fourth gear early in the race and was rather large for the narrow Italian roads that made up much of the course.

◉ At the Nürburgring, the Hobbs/Surtees Lola-Aston Martin qualified second fastest to the Spence/Hill Chaparral 2F. During the race, a wheel fell off while Hobbs was driving, and finally the rear suspension broke while Surtees was running in seventh place overall.

"At the Nürburgring we were right in there from the beginning. We qualified second overall and got away slowly but safely at the start. We were running comfortably in seventh place when the rear suspension broke, putting us out of the race. The engine performed very well and we showed real promise for Le Mans." —John Surtees

"I drove the Lola-Aston Martin in 1967, and I did a lot of the testing on that car. There was always a constant battle between Lola and Aston Martin because the car was an absolute pig in a straight line. We went to the Nürburgring and a wheel came off while I was driving, and the suspension broke while John was driving. We were in serious contention before those incidents occurred." —David Hobbs

◉ When the Lola-Aston Martins lined up in front of their Le Mans pit boxes on race day, expectations ran high. Little did anyone realize that disaster was about to strike.

◉ First lap and John Surtees (11) leads the Ickx/Muir Gulf Mirage (15) past the pits. Two laps later, Surtees would be in the pits with a holed piston.

"It was at Le Mans that the whole Lola-Aston Martin project died. It was a totally and utterly stupid thing that killed what could have been a very successful venture. Aston Martin didn't keep their feet on the ground, and they actually made changes to the engine that had never been tested. We were running things in the engines at Le Mans that had never been tested. This is something that you just don't do. As it was, I blew a piston on the third lap, and the other car didn't get past the third hour before it blew its engine. Our effort was over before the race was four hours old because of the utter and complete stupidity on the part of the engineers at Aston Martin. The Aston Martin people were not race-oriented at that time, and they just dillydallied around and made a complete muck of things. There was no reason why the Lola-Aston Martin project couldn't have put up a very reasonable show at Le Mans. That project should have worked. I knew the Ferrari engine, and, frankly, I didn't think that we would get as much power out of the old Aston Martin V-8 engine as Ferrari had. By taking the Aston Martin engine out to 5 liters and combining it with the lighter, more effective Lola, we should have stood a good chance to do well at Le Mans. At that time there was no British involvement in long-distance racing, and we felt that we could have had real possibilities. I really wanted to have a good go at the Fords, Chaparrals, and Ferraris, but it just wasn't to be. It was one of the most disappointing times of my racing career. When we returned to England, we yanked the Aston Martin engines out of the cars and installed the Chevrolet engines, which we ran for the rest of the season." —John Surtees

◉ The Irwin/de Klerk Lola-Aston Martin fared a bit better than the Surtees/Hobbs car, but it only lasted three hours before blowing its engine.

"Our next race in the Lola-Aston Martin was at Le Mans, and that was an absolute primo disaster for us. Apparently, the brand of plugs was changed just before the race, and this caused the heat range to change. The car did only three laps before burning a piston and retiring from the race. Everyone went ballistic, and there was a huge row involving Surtees and one of the Aston mechanics over the plug change. After Le Mans, we pulled the Aston engines out, threw them away, and installed Chevrolet engines in the two cars. We went to Reims and qualified second but didn't finish. We ran really well at the BOAC 500, but we didn't finish there either. The Lola coupe was a much better car once we put the Chevy in it." —David Hobbs

◉ At the start of the May 1967 Bridgehampton USRRC, George Follmer (16) Lola T70 literally left the competition in the dust. Follmer's lead was short-lived, however, and he retired from the race with a blown engine. Mark Donohue won the race in his Sunoco Lola.

"Ah, the T70. Great car. You could drive the shit out of it, and I did. It was also one of the most beautiful race cars ever built." —George Follmer

◉ Mark Donohue (6) Lola T70 breaks into the lead at the start of the June 1967 Watkins Glen USRRC. Following Donohue are Sam Posey (2) McLaren M1A, Peter Revson (52) McLaren M1A, Lothar Motschenbacher (11) McLaren M1A, John Cannon (62) McLaren M1A, and Chuck Parsons (26) McLaren M1A. Donohue won the race and clinched the 1967 USRRC Championship for Penske Racing.

Roger Penske gives Mark Donohue a pit signal during the race that would clinch the first of many championship titles that Penske Racing would win.

A full house at the 1967 BOAC 500 (run at Brands Hatch) saw John Surtees (2) Lola-Chevrolet get the jump on Paul Hawkins (8) Ferrari 330P4 in a race to the Paddock Hill Bend. Surtees had qualified on the front row, while Hawkins had already come from fifth starting position to challenge for the lead.

◉ Mike de Udy (5) Lola-Chevrolet passes David Prophet's (57) Ferrari 250LM early in the race. De Udy suffered from various problems (a loose door and a dead battery) that ultimately forced him out of the race.

◉ The Surtees/Hobbs (2) Lola-Chevrolet pulls away from the Scarfiotti/Sutcliffe Ferrari 330P4 at Stirling's Bend. Surtee's Lola would not finish the race.

◎ The Surtees/Hobbs (2) Lola-Chevrolet leads the Hill/Spence (1) Chaparral 2F (eventual race winner) toward Druids Bend. The Lola ran well when it ran, but it was bothered by carburetor problems and finally a blown engine.

"Those Lolas were really fabulous cars. In the beginning, John Surtees, Denny Hulme, David Hobbs, and Hugh Dibley had great success in the UK with the T70, and it really worried all of the rest of us who were running the other brands. We were always worried about the Lolas because they had so much tremendous potential in the shorter races, but in the longer races we never considered them much a threat because they would sit on the pole in qualifying and fall by the wayside in the race. The Ford and Chevrolet engines that we got in the UK at that time just weren't sorted out yet." —David Piper

◎ The 1967 Penske Racing Can-Am teammates, Mark Donohue (6) and George Follmer (16), race their T70s past a huge crowd of fans at Road America. Donohue finished second in his Mk.3B and Follmer finished 18th in his Mk.3.

George Follmer (16) and John Surtees (7) ran in the top 10 before Follmer had trouble. Surtees finished second.

"I got the ride with Roger Penske because I had driven against Donohue in the 1967 USRRC, and I was always as fast or faster than he was. When Roger decided to run two cars in the 1967 Can-Am, he called me. I did not like the Mk.3 Lolas because I felt that they were a step backward from my old Mk.2. I always felt that my car was faster and that it suited me better than Roger's."
—George Follmer

Dan Gurney (36) Lola T70 Mk.3B gets a good jump on the field at the 1967 Bridgehampton Cam-Am. Following Gurney are Denny Hulme (5) McLaren M6A, Bruce McLaren (4) McLaren M6A, Jim Hall (66) Chaparral 2G, George Follmer (16) Lola T70 Mk.3, Mark Donohue (6) Lola T70 Mk.3B, and John Surtees (7) Lola T70 Mk.3B. Gurney DNFed, and Follmer was the highest placed Lola, finishing in third position. The McLarens were taking over, and the Lolas were on their way out.

An always courteous Dan Gurney takes time out from his race preparation to sign a Polaroid photograph for a pretty race fan. You're much less likely to see this happen with today's drivers.

◉ Dan Gurney (36) leads a field of legends toward the very fast Turn 3 at Laguna Seca in October 1967. Close behind Gurney are Bruce McLaren (4) McLaren M6A, Parnelli Jones (21) Lola T70, Denny Hulme (5) McLaren M6A, Mike Spence (22) McLaren M1B, Jim Hall (66) Chaparral 2G, Charlie Hayes (25) McKee Mk.7, Lothar Motschenbacher (11) Lola T70, Peter Revson (52) Lola T70 Mk.3B, George Follmer (16) Lola T70 Mk.3, and John Surtees (7) Lola T70 Mk.3B.

◉ Lothar Motschenbacher (11) Lola T70 leads a group of Lolas out of Turn 2 at Laguna Seca. Peter Revson (52) Lola T70 Mk.3B, Mark Donohue (6) Lola T70 Mk.3B, George Follmer (16) Lola T70 Mk.3, Chuck Parsons (26) McLaren M1C, and John Surtees (7) Lola T70 Mk.3B give chase.

"I drove a Lola T70 for Dana Chevrolet in the 1967 Can-Am. I liked the roadster, but by that time, it was much too heavy. Overall, I did like the car, although its characteristics were quite different from those of the McLarens that I had been driving for the past two years. We didn't have any testing time in the Lola, and it showed when we went to the races. Those cars were very strong, and we didn't break things. Out of the box, they were one of the best cars of the era. The one good thing about Lola was, good or bad, you could always buy that year's car. You never could do that with the McLaren. The Lola Mk. 3 roadsters were too heavy, but at least Broadley delivered a sound, safe car to his customers. It was up to you to make any changes and modifications." —Lothar Motschenbacher

◉ Dan Gurney (36) qualified for the pole position at the 1967 Riverside Can-Am with his much modified Lola T70 Mk.3B. Gurney led the first three laps before engine failure forced him to retire from the race. Following Gurney through Turn 7 are Bruce McLaren (4) McLaren M6A, Jim Hall (66) Chaparral 2G, and Parnelli Jones (21) Lola T70.

"One of the proudest moments of my racing career was winning the pole position at the 1967 Times Grand Prix in our Ford-powered Lola T70. I beat out some pretty illustrious names for that honor, but my only problem was that I blew the engine after leading the race for just three laps."
—Dan Gurney

◉ Parnelli Jones (21) Lola T70 and Bruce McLaren (4) McLaren M6A stage a crowd-pleasing, no-holds-barred race. Jones finished fourth overall driving the George Bignotti–prepared Lola powered by the Indianapolis Ford twin-cam engine. McLaren won the race.

"We never won any races with that car [Bignotti Lola], but once we got the bugs out of the engine, it was damn quick. We had a little trouble with the car at first because that engine was not built to run on gasoline, and it kept vapor locking. Once George got that corrected, it was a really neat car. That engine was great on the road courses, and I wish we could have run it more because it had a lot of potential. That Lola was sure beautiful, and it was really easy to drive. It was a great piece of equipment, and it was the right combination." —Parnelli Jones

◉ The de Udy/Dibley Lola qualified fifth fastest for the Kyalami 9-Hour Race in October 1967. De Udy lead the race for a while against tremendous competition from the Lolas of Paul Hawkins, Roy Pierpoint, Mike Spence, Frank Gardner, Doug Serrurier, and Jackie Pretorius. The de Udy/Dibley Lola retired from the race with mechanical woes, and the Jacky Ickx/Brian Redman Gulf Mirage was the overall winner.

◉ At the Las Vegas Can-Am, Parnelli Jones (21) Lola T70 got a disputed flying start and took the lead going into the first corner. That lead was short-lived, however, as Jones retired after four laps with gearshift problems. Denis Hulme (5) McLaren M6A, Bruce McLaren (4) M6A, Jim Hall (66) Chaparral 2G, and Peter Revson (52) Lola T70 chase Jones.

"We were long gone in the 1967 Stardust Can-Am when the gearshift lever broke off in my hand and put us out of the race after only four laps. We had finally gotten the bugs out of that car, and it was really fast that day." —Parnelli Jones

◉ John Surtees wins the final Can-Am race for the Lola T70 at Las Vegas.

"In 1967, we ran into a disaster with our aluminum Chevrolet engines. We figured that in order to counteract the works programs that Chaparral and McLaren had, we ought to do something, and, rather foolishly, we went to Weslake. We tried to build an even more advanced cylinder head than the rest of the teams, and that was absolutely disastrous. Our engine problems also coincided with the coming of the Lola T70 Mk. III, which was not a very good car. In fact, the only Cam-Am race that I won in 1967 was when I switched back to my original 1966 car and engine package. I repeated my win in the final event of the year at Las Vegas, and I did it with the same car that I had driven the year before. I had that car for sale with Carl Haas, and I was lucky enough to be able to get it off of him for that race." —John Surtees

CHAPTER 3

NEW LIFE AND A DOWNHILL SLIDE 1968-1970

The new FIA rules in 1968 favored the Lola coupes (and Ford GTs) because a number of T70s existed already. The Group 6 cars would be the prototypes of which less than 50 had been built and would be restricted to 3.0 liters. The Group 4 cars would need to prove that 50 examples had been built in order to be homologated for that class and would run 5.0-liter engines. Broadley realized that by 1968 he had built almost 50 T70s, if you combined both the roadsters and the coupes. If one used the logic that Shelby American, Ferrari, Aston Martin, and Jaguar had used in the past, then Group 4 homologation with the Chevrolet 5.0-liter engine was a slam dunk. All bets were off for the 1969 season, however, when the Group 6 homolagation rules were changed. With requirements reduced to 25 cars, Porsche's 917 and Ferrari's 512 were able to compete in Group 6.

The Lola coupes were homologated by the March 1968 Sebring race, but they proved no match for the Porsche 908, Gulf Ford GT40, Porsche 917, and Ferrari 312 in the 1968 and 1969 World Championship races. In the British Championships, in nonchampionship racing on the continent, and in South Africa, the Lola coupes were very competitive in the hands of drivers such as Denis Hulme, Brian Redman, Jo Bonnier, Mike de Udy, David Piper, Chris Craft, and Frank Gardner. Eric Broadley remembers, "The coupes became very successful after they were equipped with the 5.0-liter Chevrolet engines. We had a couple of good years with those cars, but we were overtaken by the Porsche 917s and the Ferrari 512s. Our aerodynamics were better than Porsche's in the beginning, but when they caught up, we were in serious trouble. We missed some great opportunities, but we had too many commitments in other areas to pin ourselves down."

It was at Daytona in February 1969 that Roger Penske's Sunoco Lola T70 Mk.3B coupe shocked the motor racing world with, what was at the time, the most unbelievable upset in recent endurance racing history. Porsche came to the race as the overwhelming favorite, but mechanical problems (split exhaust manifolds and broken intermediate shafts) forced the five factory 908s to retire from the race. The two John Wyer Gulf Ford GT40 entries were front-runners, but one crashed and the other suffered overheating problems. This turn of events opened the door for the Lola to

◉ **Chuck Parsons (10) Lola T163 and Jackie Oliver (22) T122 lap Bob Nagel (24) Lola T70 in Turn 7 at Riverside. Parsons drove a brand new T163 to a fine second-place finish.**

"In my opinion, the best car that Lola ever made was the T163 that I ran at Riverside in 1969. The car was pretty damn good before, but once we got some things fixed and got a big-block aluminum Chevrolet engine, that Lola was absolutely fantastic. The car just hauled ass on the long Riverside straight, and I must have passed 10 cars on one lap early in the race. Before the 1969 season started, the McLaren team did a lot of testing, and Lola didn't. That lack of testing showed up in our early season results. We'd get a car one week and go racing with it the next. With an 11-race series, there was never any time to sort out the car between races. The Can-Am was the best racing series ever devised, but the politics ruined it. I think when the turbo Porsches came in, the whole series went downhill in a hurry." —Chuck Parsons

win its first and only FIA endurance race, but it wouldn't be an easy road. The Penske Lola had some major troubles of its own with a broken exhaust system and a serious fuel pickup problem, but the team persevered long enough to prove once again that you had to survive to finish, and you had to finish to win. Although the Lola had better aerodynamics than Porsche in the beginning, Porsche mounted a serious factory effort that resulted in a lighter, more reliable car with outstanding aerodynamics and tremendous power. That car was, of course, the incredible 917, which became dominant during the 1970 and 1971 seasons.

One of those areas was the Can-Am series, and the Lola T160 was introduced as the next-generation Lola Can-Am car in 1968. Quite a few of these cars were sold to American teams through the new North American distributor Carl Haas, but only two arrived in time for the opening round of the 1968 Can-Am season at Road America.

The T160 proved to be grossly inferior to the McLaren M8A, and all of the drivers (except Sam Posey) hated the car because of its weight and poor handling. No races were won using the T160, and the best finishes of the year for that car were three fourth places by Sam Posey, Swede Savage, and Chuck Parsons. It is interesting to note that the best 1968 Can-Am finish by a Lola was a second place at Las Vegas by George Follmer in a very well-used T70.

The Lola T163 was introduced to the Can-Am in 1969, and this car proved to be much more competitive than the previous year's T160. Chuck Parsons and Peter Revson drove the T163 to some reasonable finishes (Parsons had three thirds and one second), but the car wasn't in the same league as the McLaren M8Bs, which dominated the 1969 series winning all 11 races.

For 1970, Lola built the T220, but once again the car, even with Peter Revson driving, was no match for the McLaren M8D, and no races were won.

By 1970, the Lola T70 coupes were dinosaurs completely unable to compete with the front-runners in World Championship events. It was as if Lola's time to bid farewell had come, but a new Can-Am car would possibly prove that Lola still had what it took to be competitive in big-bore racing.

Eric Broadley hoped that the Lola T160 would become the successor to the very successful three-year-old model T70. It wasn't to be.

⊙ It was hoped that the T160 would challenge the McLarens for dominance in the Can-Am series, but a lack of testing and development led to a very disappointing season in 1968.

◉ John Surtees did some testing at Goodwood, but came away less than impressed.

"The 1968 Lola T160 was a terrible car, and it led to a parting of the ways between myself and Eric Broadley. By 1968, Eric had gotten sidetracked with other projects, and the Lola Can-Am cars went in the wrong direction. We had done almost no development work on the new car as we had in the past, and we just took delivery of those cars as they were built. Lola really didn't take the time to sort out the T160 before delivering the completed cars to the waiting American customers. That was a stupid mistake. The Lolas of 1967 and 1968 were not developed like the cars that we ran in 1965 and 1966. The early Lola T70 was always a bit fragile, but the development work that we did on it initially made the car come around quite successfully. After 1966, the development program got off track because there were too many changes taking place at Lola Cars. Because there was no longer any substantial Can-Am development program, the close relationship that had existed between Eric and myself became a thing of the past. If you were going to have a proper Can-Am program, you had to have the attitude that prevailed at McLaren. They had the right attitude and the right development program, and that's why they were so successful for so long in that series." —John Surtees

◉ There were no Lolas at Daytona in 1968, but four of the T70 coupes showed up at Sebring in March. Two of those cars belonged to actor James Garner's American International Racing and made their racing debut at Sebring. Here the two AIR cars undergo race preparation in the shop prior to the race. The Patrick/Jordan (9) Lola sits in the foreground, and the Leslie/Guldstrand Lola sits in the background, stripped of its bodywork.

"The first Lola that I ever drove was the T70 coupe that we ran at Sebring in 1968 for Jim Garner's team, American International Racing. I got involved with Garner's team through Scooter Patrick who knew Jim very well. Sebring was a disaster, and I never drove the car in the race because the clutch blew after only 12 laps. My co-drivers were Dick Guldstrand and Lothar Motschenbacher, but I don't remember who started the race." —Ed Leslie

COLOR GALLERY

The Pabst/Hansgen Lola GT-Chevrolet rounds the Sebring hairpin early in the March 1964 race.

Augie Pabst races along the very beautiful Road America circuit during the September 1964 500-mile race.

This may be the only color photograph in existence of John Surtees conducting some of the first Lola T70 tests at Silverstone in early 1965.

"I did most of the testing on the T70, and I felt that we had a very capable car by the time we went to the first race at Silverstone. I finished second to Jim Clark in that race, which was run in a torrential rain. Eric and myself had a very good relationship. We could relate to each other and we respected each other, and it all worked very well. In many ways I wish that we could have maintained that relationship, but other things, unfortunately, got in the way." —John Surtees

At the Players 200 in June 1965, John Surtees (11) Lola T70 and Jim Hall (66) Chaparral 2 staged one of the great crowd-pleasing races of the season. These two drivers raced like this to the finish, finishing in this order. This was the first major win for the Lola T70 and one of the few losses for the Chaparral 2 that year.

◉ Hugh P. K. Dibley bought one of the first four Lola T70s built and took it to Canada to race at Mosport in June 1965.

"I really liked the Lola people, and that helped influence me to buy one of the early T70s. When the Lola T70 came out, it was the best of the lot, and when I ordered the car I was originally going to go with the lightweight Oldsmobile engine. When I saw the size of the car, I changed my mind and ordered the car with a Traco Chevrolet. John Surtees and I took the T70 to Mosport in June 1965 for the Players 200. That was a success for Lola but not for me. In 1966, I won the support race for the British Grand Prix, and that was one of my better races in the Lola T70." —Hugh P. K. Dibley

◉ John Surtees wins the Guards Trophy at Brands Hatch in August 1965.

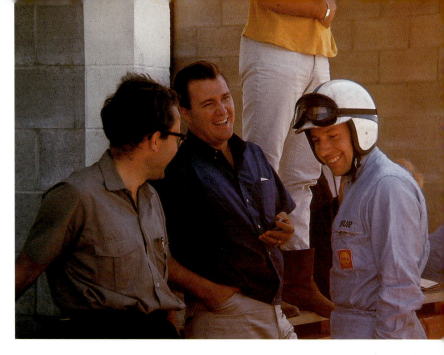

◉ Eric Broadley (left), John Mecom (center), and John Surtees (right) enjoy a laugh at Mosport in June 1965.

◉ David Hobbs brought the beautiful Harold Young Lola to North America in fall 1965. At Mosport, in September, Hobbs qualified third and was running in third position before mechanical problems forced him out of the race.

"The real disaster happened with the Harold Young Lola when we went to do the professional races in North America. In our first race, we retired at Mosport after qualifying and running in third spot. At St. Jovite the next week, we had a good effort and we finished third. After St. Jovite, it was downhill all the way. We went to Kent, Washington, and didn't finish, then on to Laguna Seca where we didn't start, and finally to Riverside where we cooked the clutch waiting for a start that became a shambles. After Riverside, everything fell completely apart, and I never drove that car again." —David Hobbs

◉ Dan Gurney became the first American driver to win a Can-Am race when he won at Bridgehampton in September 1966.

◉ John Surtees, on his way to the win in the 1966 Times Grand Prix at Riverside and the 1966 Can-Am championship, proved that a successful and winning effort could be mounted on a small budget.

◉ Mario Andretti (1) Lola T70 drove the 427-cubic-inch Ford-powered Lola at Riverside in October 1966. This car also used a semi-automatic transmission. Andretti blew the engine on the 37th lap. Jackie Stewart (43) Lola T70 and Bruce McLaren (4) McLaren M1B are behind Andretti.

"I worked on the Lola, at Riverside, that came out of Kar Kraft for Mario Andretti to drive. That car had a 427-cubic-inch engine in it, and it had a torque converter and a two-speed jump box for a transmission. Contrary to popular belief, there was never an automatic transmission involved with that car." —Max Kelly

◉ Scooter Patrick made a rare Can-Am appearance at the 1966 Times Grand Prix substituting for Hugh P. K. Dibley in the SMART Lola T70.

"I drove Hugh Dibley's T70 roadster at Riverside in 1966, and I was doing very well until the rear end broke and put me out of the race. The Lola T70s were very competitive cars, and they were better than anything else that was available for the teams to purchase at that time. We had a lot of fun in those days, and we had really good people racing and working on our cars." —Scooter Patrick

◉ Parnelli Jones was one of the hardest-charging drivers who ever strapped into a Lola T70. Jones always regretted that his busy racing schedule didn't allow for more time to race in the Can-Am series.

◉ In 1967, Mark Donohue had a brand new Lola T70 Mk.3 to race in the USRRC. At Las Vegas, Donohue started off the season with a win.

◉ Mark Donohue and the Penske Racing Sunoco Special became one of the most famous and winning Lola T70s of all time.

◎ George Follmer had the fastest car in the 1967 USRRC, but he couldn't finish a race.

"The T70 was one of those rare cars that anyone with a little experience and a little talent could get in and go fast. George Follmer had a lot of talent, a lot of experience, and he went very fast." —Bruce Burness

◎ At the Riverside USRRC, Donohue accepted the winner's champagne as the world-famous super model Twiggy (right) holds the trophy.

101

When John Surtees and the Lola-Aston Martin left the Le Mans Trials in April 1967, there was reason for optimism. Surtees had set the third fastest overall time for the weekend, including the fastest time in the rain.

At the Nürburgring in May 1967, the Surtees/Hobbs (1) Lola-Aston Martin posted the second fastest qualifying time, ran well in the race, but retired with a broken suspension on the eighth lap while running in seventh position.

The Irwin/de Klerk (12) Lola-Aston Martin was never in contention at Le Mans in June 1967. A blown engine put the car out of the race in the fourth hour.

Mark Donohue, with crew chief Karl Kainhofer, clinched the 1967 USRRC title at Watkins Glen in July 1967. Donohue won five of the seven races scheduled that year.

◎ Lothar Motschenbacher drove one of the Dana Chevrolet Lola T70s during the 1967 Can-Am series. Motschenbacher's highest finish in 1967 was fifth at Bridgehampton.

◎ Well-known USAC oval-track star driver Roger McCluskey drove the wildly painted Pacesetter Homes Lola in the 1967 Can-Am. McCluskey had little experience in sports cars, but, like many drivers of that era, he was capable of driving anything that had wheels on it.

◎ Peter Revson drove the other Dana Chevrolet Lola in the 1967 Can-Am. Revson's highest placing in 1967 was a fourth at Mosport.

◎ The 1968 Sebring race saw the debut of Jim Garner's AIR team Lolas. The Patrick/Jordan (9) Lola lasted the longest of the two cars, but blew an engine after eight hours of racing.

"I got involved with Jim Garner's AIR team through John Crean who was the owner of AIR. I really don't know how my name came about, but Jim and I had known each other from off-road racing, and I kind of fell into a driving position when the team was started. Ed Leslie, Lothar Motschenbacher, and Dave Jordan also came to the team at a later time. We had some teething problems with the Lolas at Sebring in 1968, but that was because they were brand new and untested. We had a pretty competent team working with us, and we were able to solve enough problems that I was able to set a track record that year [1968] at Sebring. Both years [1968 and 1969] at Sebring we were plagued with terrible engines, and I never finished the race in either of those two years." —Scooter Patrick

◉ Peter Revson drove a Shelby Racing Company Lola T70 in several races during the 1968 USRRC.

"When we were at Shelby Racing in 1968, we had four or five Lola T70s in our shop. We had the car that Andretti drove at Nassau in 1966 and we had a Dana Chevrolet Lola, and that's the one that Peter Revson drove at Mexico City and Riverside in the 1968 USRRC. We also had the two Sunoco cars that were run by Penske in 1967. We ran one of the Penske cars with a 427-cubic-inch Ford at the 1968 Kent USRRC where Revson put it on the pole, led one lap, and pitted with engine problems. That car went to Charlie Agapiou, and George Follmer drove it for Folger Ford in the West Coast races of the 1968 Can-Am series. We used those Lolas to test engines and different suspension settings for future Shelby projects."
—John Collins

◉ In 1968, Carl Haas became the Lola importer for North America, and his Simoniz T70s were the first of many Lolas that would be raced by his racing team over a 28-year [1968 to 1996] period. Skip Scott (26) and Chuck Parsons were the first in a long line of well-known drivers to pilot the Haas team Lolas.

◉ The Bonnier/Axelsson (11) Lola leads the Locke/Bailey (14) Porsche 906 at the July 1968 Watkins Glen 6-Hour Race. The Lola coupe qualified sixth and finished 10th overall.

◉ The 1968 Le Mans race was run in September and the Epstein/Nelson Lola qualified 16th, but various mechanical problems put the car out of the race in the 16th hour.

◉ Chuck Parsons (10) Lola T160 leads Swede Savage (36) Lola T160 and Skip Scott (26) Lola T160 during the 1968 Edmonton Can-Am race. Parsons finished fifth, Scott finished eighth, and Savage DNFed.

◉ At Daytona in February 1969, the Donohue/Parsons (9) Sunoco Lola qualified second to the Porsche 908 of Elford/Redman (52). Behind the front row are the Porsche 908s of Siffert/Herrmann (50), Stommelen/Aherns (54), Attwood/Buzzetta (51), and Mitter/Schutz (53). The Lola (60) of Bonnier/Norinder is also in the front of the field. The Gulf GT40 (2) of Hobbs/Hailwood is being pushed through the starting field to its position in the fifth row.

◉ The Patrick/Jordan (9) Lola leads the Soler-Roig/Lins/Toivonen (58) Porsche 907 and the Posey/Rodriguez (41) Ferrari 275 GTB late in the afternoon at Daytona. The AIR Lola finished seventh overall.

"Dave Jordan and myself finished seventh at Daytona in 1969, and that was the only race that I ever finished in one of the AIR Lola coupes. I really enjoyed driving those cars even though my luck was for shit when I did drive them." —Scooter Patrick

◉ On its way to a second place overall at Daytona, the Leslie/Motschenbacher (8) Lola laps the Kleinpeter/Beatty/Gunn (39) Chevron-BMW B8. The Chevron finished sixth overall.

"Scooter Patrick was a very close friend of Jim Garner, and I was a friend of Scooter's. That's how I got picked to be on the AIR team for the 1968 and 1969 seasons." —Ed Leslie

105

The Sunoco Lola's road to victory at Daytona was not an easy one for the Penske team. A 1-hour and 19-minute night pit stop to repair a broken exhaust header was just one of the problems that the team faced on its way to a huge upset win.

Nighttime affords the intrepid photographer a chance to capture some incredible images. Here, the Leslie/Motschenbacher Lola undergoes a scheduled pit stop on a cold Daytona night.

◉ The Donohue/Parsons Sunoco Lola races to victory at Daytona in February 1969. It is interesting to note that of all of the models that have been made of this car, no one has ever gotten the striping correct on the final product. And no model has ever had the flames that appear on the deck lid in front of the number on its decal sheet. Why?

◉ The Penske crew pushes the Donohue/Bucknum Sunoco Lola to its starting position for the March 1969 Sebring race.

◉ The sixth-place finishing AIR Lola, driven by Ed Leslie and Lothar Motschenbacher, undergoes brake service during a night pit stop at Sebring.

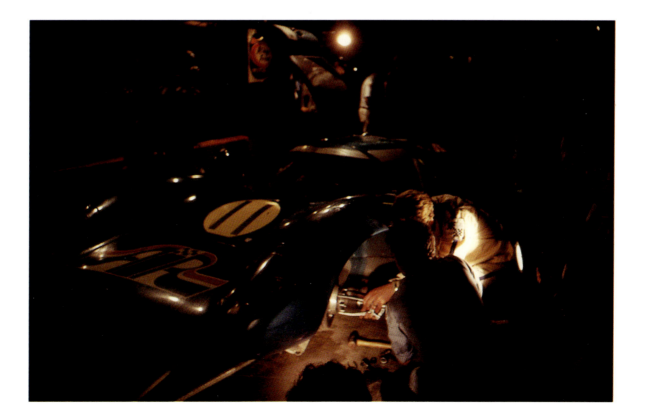

◉ The Hawkins/Prophet/Piper Lola finished eighth at the 1969 Spa 1,000 km in spite of a blown engine near the finish of the race.

"The T70 coupe was a fabulous car to drive, but I was always frustrated by the cylinder head problem that we could never seem to cure. The T70 coupe was a beautiful car to look at, and even by today's standards, it doesn't disgrace itself. The pedal pressures were light, the steering was great, and you always wanted to drive it again." —David Piper

◉ The day after the July 1969 Watkins Glen Six-Hour Race, Jo Bonnier (19) appeared on the starting grid for the Can-Am race. Here, on his way to a seventh overall placing, Bonnier leads George Eaton (98) McLaren M12, Tony Dean 914) Porsche 908, and Chris Amon (16) Ferrari 612P.

◉ Chuck Parsons in the beautiful Simoniz Lola T163 at the October 1969 Riverside Can-Am.

Teddy Pilette and Gustave Gosselin started the only Lola to qualify for the 1970 Le Mans race. After qualifying 27th, the Lola ran as high as third overall before gearbox problems eliminated the car from the race after nine hours.

Jacques Rey wins his class at the beautiful Turckheim-Trios Epis hillclimb in June 1970.

Jacques Rey certainly picked some beautiful places at which to compete with his Lola coupe. Rey finished first in class at this hillclimb in Bellegrade in August 1970.

Peter Revson qualified third fastest for the October 1970 Riverside Can-Am but was put out of the race after only eight laps with overheating problems.

Jackie Stewart put the fear of God in the McLaren team during the 1971 Can-Am season with his Lola T260. Unfortunately, a lack of proper handling and various mechanical malfunctions prevented Stewart's effort from becoming all that it might have been. Many hoped that the T260 would be the car that would finally break the McLaren domination of the series, but it was not to be.

Jackie Stewart enters Riverside's Turn 6 during the October 1971 Can-Am race. Even with the rear wing set back and the "cow catcher" attached, the T260 was still an ill-handling brute.

David Hobbs finishes fourth overall at the July 1972 Watkins Glen Can-Am.

Bob Nagel (17) Lola T260 leads Vic Elford (102) Shadow DN2 Turbo Chevrolet, Steve Durst (11) McLaren M8F, and Charlie Kemp (23) Porsche 917/10K down the famed corkscrew during the October 1973 Laguna Seca Can-Am.

◉ The 1973 Laguna Seca Can-Am afforded a chance to catch a rare photograph of the two Lola T260s running together. Bob Nagel (17) leads John Gunn (39) out of Turn 9. Nagel finished sixth, while Gunn had fuel injection problems on the 23rd lap.

◉ Bob Nagel finished fourth at the Watkins Glen Can-Am in July 1974. A month later the Can-Am, as we knew it, would run its final race at Road America.

◉ Three of the four Lolas entered at Sebring can be seen in this picture if you look carefully. The de Udy/Dibley (11) Lola T70 coupe gets a great start as the Bonnier/Axelsson (10) Lola T70 coupe and the Patrick/Jordan (9) Lola T70 coupe prepare to leave the line. The Leslie/Guldstrand (8) Lola T70 coupe started well back in 34th position. None of these Lolas finished the race. Others in the picture are Vic Elford (51) Porsche 907, Jacky Ickx (28) Ford GT40, David Hobbs (29) Ford GT40, Horst Kwech (32) Shelby Mustang, Gerhard Mitter (48) Porsche 907, Karl Foitek (56) Porsche 910, and Mauro Bianchi (42) Renault Alpine.

"I drove a Lola coupe for Jim Garner's AIR racing team at Sebring in 1968. I got the ride because I had done some work with Garner on the movie Grand Prix, and we all became pretty good friends. Jim wanted to continue racing after the movie was finished, so Bob Bondurant and myself set up a company that we called American International Racing. We originally bought and raced Corvettes, then we bought the Lola T70 coupes. The first time that we ran the Lolas was at Sebring in March 1968, and we continued to use those cars at Daytona and Sebring in 1969. I only drove those cars at Sebring in 1968, and after that I was racing team manager for a while. The T70 was a great car, and it was much easier to drive than any of the McLarens that I ever drove. The car was very predictable, and you could really stand on it. Those coupes were really beautiful. The coupe was a super car, but we were hampered with a small-block Chevrolet engine. We were going through the sorting out process at Sebring in 1968. We got those cars right off the plane from England at Orlando airport, and we had no time to check out or test anything before the race. We were literally building those cars on the trailers back to Sebring. We had suspension problems, gearbox problems, and numerous other problems at Sebring, but we didn't have the time to fix them. We had a very good crew and a good team, but time was against us there. Those coupes were well designed, but they were very fragile." —Dick Guldstrand

In 1968, the Lolas had a much more productive season in England than in North America or in the world championship endurance races. Denny Hulme, Brian Redman, and Frank Gardner drove the Sidney Taylor Lolas to a number of wins in England, including this one by Denny Hulme at the Silverstone Players Trophy Race in April 1968.

"In 1968, we could buy a complete Lola coupe with a Chevrolet engine and a spare set of wheels for £4,000. I had a lot of great drivers with me in both the roadsters and coupes. Denny Hulme, Frank Gardner, Brian Redman, Jack Brabham, and Peter Revson were but a few of my drivers at that time. I enjoyed running the coupes, and they were a really lovely car. It was a properly finished car; easy to run, and it had very good lines. The aerodynamics were quite good, and Lola Cars was a fantastic company to work with." —Sidney Taylor

The Norinder/Widdows Lola qualified 12th at the Nürburgring in May 1968, but blew the engine early in the race.

At Spa, the Epstein/Liddell Lola finished 10th overall despite low oil-pressure problems.

The Bonnier/Axelsson/Parsons (11) Lola coupe seems a bit outnumbered by the four Porsche 908s, two Gulf Ford GT40s, and two Howmet Turbines at the 1968 Watkins Glen 6-Hour. Bonnier qualified sixth, worked his way up to third, and fell back with transmission problems to finish 10th.

◉ By 1968, Carl Haas had become the Lola Importer for North America, and his Simoniz team ran the rather outdated Lola T70s in the USRRC. Chuck Parsons (10) leads teammate Skip Scott (26) at Watkins Glen in July 1968. Parsons finished second and Scott DNFed.

"By the time I first drove a Lola T70 in 1968, those cars were a thing of the past. At that time they were just too big and heavy to be competitive. I joined the Carl Haas Simoniz team in 1968, and we used the T70 in the USRRC series that year. By that time, McLaren had developed the M6 series cars and they were much better than the Lolas. Mark Donohue and Roger Penske had Bruce McLaren's M6A championship car from the 1967 Can-Am, and they made fools of all of us in that final year of the USRRC series." —Chuck Parsons

◉ Jo Bonnier (2) leads Denny Hulme (1) during the Martini Trophy race at Silverstone in July 1968. Hulme won the race by two laps, while Bonnier succumbed to lack of oil pressure.

Mike de Udy (47) and Jo Bonnier (49) race nose-to-tail during the August 1968 Speedworld International Trophy race at Oulton Park. De Udy and Bonnier raced this way the entire distance, finishing in this order.

Paul Hawkins (46) finished third to complete the Lola sweep at the Speedworld International Trophy. Hawkins leads Chris Craft's (36) Tech-Speed Chevron, which finished fifth overall.

At the September 1968 Road America Can-Am, Mario Andretti qualified eighth fastest in his first race in the George Bignotti Lola that Parnelli Jones had driven in the previous season. Unfortunately, the Ford DOHC engine blew early in the race.

"The first Lola T70 that I ever drove was for Eric Broadley at Riverside in 1965. In those days, the Lola was the state of the art, and I had never been in anything like that before. I really felt like a fish out of water. Eric really had something special, and because of that, the car immediately became likable. The T70 was very pleasing to look at, and it was mechanically sound. When I got in the car, it felt very foreign to me because I had never sat in the car or tested in the car before I first saw it at Riverside. Les Richter had gotten me some starting money and Lola provided the car, but it was a last-minute deal and it wasn't a very good effort. The Lola T70 that I drove for George Bignotti in 1968 probably had the most potential and was the most fun of any of those cars that I ever drove. George was always coming up with something new, and we did do some testing and some preparing so that we knew what to expect when we got to the track. That project, unfortunately, was short-lived because it didn't have enough money to keep running." —Mario Andretti

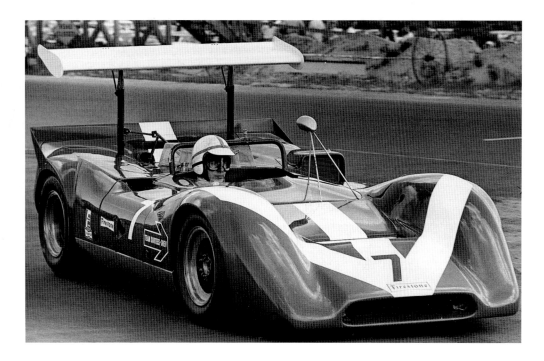

John Surtees joined the Can-Am series at Bridgehampton with a much-modified Lola T160 dubbed the "TS Chevrolet." Surtees' modifications included chassis lightening, suspension revisions, and the addition of a Chaparral-style wing. None of it worked however, and the season turned out to be a complete disaster. Surtees' engine blew early in the race after he qualified 10th.

◉ The Carl Haas Simoniz team ran the Lola T160 for the 1968 Can-Am season. Parsons had a very disappointing season in a car he didn't like.

"The Simoniz team switched to the Lola because with McLaren you could never get the latest car. Everything was always last season's car. For the 1968 Can-Am, we ran the T160s and they were absolutely terrible." —Chuck Parsons

◉ After driving a McLaren and a Caldwell, Sam Posey was the only driver who actually liked driving the Lola T160.

"I drove a Lola T160 in the 1968 Can-Am series, and I wish we'd had that car a little earlier so that we could have really sorted it out quicker. Once the bugs were worked out, it was a wonderful car. I only raced that car six times [five Can-Am races and once in Japan at the end of the season], and my first race in the T160 was at Bridgehampton, which was the second race of the six-race season. I loved that car, and once we got a 427-cubic inch, aluminum Chevrolet engine, the Lola just flat flew. My best race with the T160 was at Las Vegas when we were running third with about five laps to go. We were ready for a podium finish when we accidentally ran out of gas. In spite of that problem, we still finished fifth. After three years of running in the Can-Am, we were finally on the knife's edge, and it was all because of that car. When I started racing in the Can-Am, I had a choice of going with a McLaren or a Lola chassis and a Chevy or a Ford engine, and I picked wrong in both cases." —Sam Posey

○ In 1968, due to French political problems, Le Mans was run at the end of September. The Epstein/Nelson (6) Lola leads the Alfa Romeo T33/2 (39) of Giunti and Galli through the esses early in the race. The Lola ran as high as fifth before falling back with numerous mechanical problems and dropping out of the race. The Alfa finished fourth overall.

○ John Surtees' (7) Lola T160 blows an engine as he leads Sam Posey (1) Lola T160, Charlie Hayes (25) McKee Mk.8, Jerry Titus (17) McLaren M6B, and John Cordts (57) McLaren M1C at the Edmonton Can-Am.

◎ Jackie Epstein (103) Lola T70 coupe leads Jackie Oliver (142) Lotus 47, David Piper (115) Ferrari 250LM, and Edward Nelson (110) Ford GT40 at the Guards Trophy at Brands Hatch in September 1968. Frank Gardner won the race in the Sid Taylor Lola.

◎ The first time that a Lola coupe appeared in a Can-Am race was at Laguna Seca in October 1968. Ed Leslie (18) shows signs of contact during the very wet race as he laps Jerry Entin (12) Lola T70 at Turn 9.

"I ran the Harvey Snow Lola T70 coupe in the Can-Am races at Laguna Seca, Riverside, and Las Vegas. Harvey was an enthusiast, not a racer, and I didn't see his team as being a very serious effort until it started to rain at Laguna Seca. It was at that time that I got serious because I thought that we had a real chance to win. I loved Laguna Seca because it was my home track, and I went out there with the idea that we could possibly finish in the money. We didn't have a very good engine, and we had lousy tires, but those lousy tires turned out to be really neat rain tires. When it started raining, I started moving up through the field, and I passed about 10 cars in 10 laps. Just as I was feeling good about my chances, the engine blew on the front straight in front of the pits and shot flames around my head. That really scared the shit out of me. That old Laguna Seca track was great in the rain, but you had to pay attention and not go flat-out in some of the places that you could in the dry." —Ed Leslie

◉ Dan Gurney split his Can-Am season between his Lola T160 and his McLeagle. Swede Savage, Gurney's protégé, drove the second car for the All American Racers' team in 1968.

"The Lola T160 was not one of the better Lolas that Eric Broadley built, although Swede Savage managed to give it a good run in the rain at Laguna Seca, at least for a while. At its worst, the T160 was better than our McLeagle, which we had managed to screw up beyond belief in the suspension department." —Dan Gurney

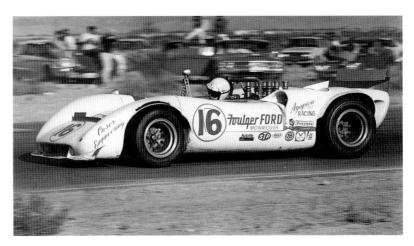

◉ This is the well-worn ex-Penske, ex-Shelby, Lola T70 Mk.3 that passed to Charlie and Kerry Agapiou at the end of the 1968 Can-Am season. George Follmer drove the car to a fine second-place finish at the November 1968 Las Vegas Can-Am.

"In 1968, I drove a Lola for the Agapiou brothers, but that car was pretty well worn out by the time that I got into it. It had been run by Penske in 1967, and it had been a test mule for Ford in early 1968. The Agapiou brothers didn't have much money to keep the car going, but they did a good job with what they had. That car was a good car in the rain at Laguna Seca because we had the Firestone rain tires. The car was very heavy, and we had a heavy Ford 427-cubic-inch engine in it. We didn't have the luxury of all of that aluminum stuff that all of the Chevy guys had access to. In those days, you either drove a Lola or you drove a McLaren; there really wasn't any other choice. Basically, if you used Firestones, you drove a Lola, and if you used Goodyears, you drove a McLaren—it was that simple. I really enjoyed driving those cars, and I have great memories of my days in them." —George Follmer

◉ The de Udy/Gardner Lola T70 coupe sits in the pits prior to the start of the November 1968 Kyalami 9-Hour Race.

"Mike de Udy and I drove a Lola coupe in South Africa, and we were able to hold off some pretty formidable people down there. John Love was a very good driver, and he had a 6.0-liter engine in his Lola. We only had a 5.0-liter engine, and we were able to hold him off. Love's car was very well prepared, and he had a good budget from the Gunston cigarette people. We ran the Lola at Kyalami, Capetown, and other places. The Lola was a car that didn't take a great deal of setting up to go quickly, and it had very good durability. I drove some cars that were real animals during my racing career, but the T70 Lola was not one of them. For several years, if you wanted to beat a T70 Lola, you needed to be driving a T70 Lola." —Frank Gardner

"In 1968, my brother and I raced a Lola T70 that we had gotten from Shelby. Prior to that, it had been one of the Sonoco cars that Penske's team ran in 1967. George Follmer drove it at Laguna Seca, Riverside, and Las Vegas. That car was extremely quick, and we had a second-place finish with it at Las Vegas. The car was very easy to work on, and Follmer drove the hell out of it. We were a little Mickey Mouse operation with no money, but with George driving, we were very competitive in a very tough series." —Charlie Agapiou

The Racing Car Show in January 1969 featured three new Lolas, including the T162 Can-Am car.

Also seen at the show was the Lola T70 Mk.3B coupe painted in the colors of Sid Taylor Racing.

Interest was shown in the prototype Lola T70 Mk.3B road car, but few if any were ever built. This car was modified by Sbarro ACA of Lausanne, Switzerland.

At Daytona in February 1969, the Bonnier/Norinder Lola T70 coupe laps the Robson/Rogers Jaguar E-type and the Drolet/Gimondo (96) Corvette at 200 miles per hour. This Lola crashed out of contention in the second hour.

The Leslie/Motschenbacher (8) AIR Lola leaves the Merello/Rose Ferrari 250LM in the dust as it races to a second-place finish.

"I once again drove the Lola T70 coupes for Jim Garner's team at Daytona and Sebring in 1969. At Daytona we finished second to the Penske Lola, but we should have won that race. The Penske car was trick all the way, and it was extremely well prepared. When the race started, it was gone. Charlie Parsons was Mark Donohue's co-driver, and he sucked the fuel tank dry when it didn't vent. From that point on, the Penske car could only go about 30 laps before it had to stop. We had a Dutch mechanic who put the gears in our Hewland gearbox out of sequence, so we had only three forward gears. When I shifted to second gear, it was perfect, but when I shifted to third, it went into fifth. The secret to Daytona was getting through the banked turns flat out, and we were doing that. The biggest problem at Daytona was that the sun got so low in certain spots at sunrise and sunset that you were blind for several hundred feet, and you just hoped that there wasn't anything in your way. The only reason we were in second at the end of the race was because we kept it going and everyone else dropped out. We should have been able to beat the Penske car, but the gears wouldn't let us have the speed to do it." —Ed Leslie

◉ Lothar Motschenbacher (left) and Jim Garner (right) review Daytona race strategy.

"At Daytona, those coupes were pretty good cars. The aerodynamics were very good, and we were able to achieve some pretty good speeds on the high banks. Our engines were pretty good; they were, I think, 365-cubic-inch Traco small-block Chevrolets." —Lothar Motschenbacher

◉ Night pit stops separate the men from the boys, and no one ever did it better than the Penske Racing crew. Nobody could have imagined that the beautiful blue Penske Lola would win the 24-hour race. More than two hours total were spent in the pits to repair a variety of mechanical problems. The most costly stop was 1 hour, 19 minutes to fix a broken exhaust header. The car also had a fuel pickup problem that made extra pit stops necessary.

◎ Mark Donohue (far left) and Chuck Parsons in Victory Lane.

"I think our win at Daytona in 1969 was one of the greatest upsets in the history of World Championship endurance racing." —Roger Penske

◉ At Sebring the AIR team sits in the pits prior to the start of the race. Ed Leslie and Lothar Motschenbacher drove the #11 Lola to sixth place overall, while the Scooter Patrick/Dave Jordan #10 Lola blew an engine 15 laps into the race.

"At Sebring we qualified sixth and finished sixth, and, once again, I had Lothar Motschenbacher as my co-driver. Lothar was a very good endurance driver because he didn't hurt the car during his driving stints. I liked those Lola coupes. They handled well, felt safe, and they were very fast when they ran correctly. The Garner team broke up because the studio was against him having a racing team, and the people that he had managing the team were not racing people and had no idea of how to run a racing team." —Ed Leslie

◉ The Penske Racing Sunoco Lola makes a well orchestrated, scheduled pit stop while Ronnie Bucknum (left) prepares to enter the car. This Lola qualified second fastest and was among the race leaders until a broken trailing arm put it out of the race after 5 hours and 37 minutes. The engine of the Sunoco Lola featured ram-tuned Lucas fuel injection instead of the Weber carburetors that all of the other Lolas used at that time.

The first race of the 1969 RAC Group 4 Championship was run at Silverstone at the end of March. Denny Hulme and his (37) John Woolfe Lola won the race, barely beating Brian Redman in his (29) Sid Taylor Lola to the finish. Seven Lolas were entered in this race, and during the 1969 season, a virtual who's who of top racing talent drove these beautiful cars when their schedules allowed it.

"In 1968 and 1969 I drove several of the Lola T70 coupes, and I found them to be very good cars. I had several wins and a number of other good results in the Lolas. I liked the coupe, but I was slightly apprehensive in the car after seeing several bad accidents that were caused by suspension failure. The Lola handled as well, or better, than the early 917s, but it couldn't compare in power and reliability. The Lola was a very good car, but they just couldn't make it last over the long haul." —Brian Redman

Eight Lolas started the BOAC 500 at Brands Hatch in April 1969. The Hawkins/Williams (1) Lola leads the Piper/Pierpoint (2) Lola, the Revson/Hulme/Axelsson (4) Lola, and the ill-fated Bonnier/Muller Lola (3) toward Stirling's Bend. Bonnier was involved in a terrible high-speed crash at Bottom Bend late in the race that necessitated all of the still-running Lolas being brought in for a suspension inspection with just one hour to go in the race.

"I co-drove David Piper's T70 coupe at the BOAC 500 in 1969. That was the time when Jo Bonnier had his huge shunt because the rear suspension failed, and all of the Lolas were withdrawn after Jo's crash. Until that time, the car was very competitive in the race. Those cars were very good with the Chevy engines. They were great cars to drive, and they were a lot of fun. I always preferred the roadster to the coupe if I had my choice. It was very quick, it handled well, and it was a very nice car." —Roy Pierpoint

◉ Peter Revson (4) Lola leads Paul Hawkins through Bottom Bend during the BOAC 500. Revson blew the engine, and Hawkins retired with rear suspension breakage.

"The Group 4 races that were run in England in 1969 were very competitive and almost everyone drove the Lola cars. When you won one of those races, you beat a lot of great people. The first trouble that we had with the T70 was with the cylinder heads cracking on the engine, and we couldn't seem to solve the problem. We also used to have some serious chassis problems with the suspension on the T70. If you remember, Jo Bonnier had a big shunt behind the pits at Brands Hatch coming out of Bottom Bend and wrote his Lola off. I was driving my Lola in that race, and Eric made me withdraw my car from the race. What had happened was that Lola had a very good welder who did all of the fabrication on the T70s, but they lost him and they got someone else to do the work. The new person wasn't welding the plugs in the end of the radius rods properly, and the plugs were pulling out, causing the rear suspension to collapse. That's what caused Bonnier's accident. The same thing happened to Peter Troberg at the Osterreichring, and it also happened to me once. We finally had to throw away all of the radius rods and make new ones. That was a very serious problem, but apart from that, the car was way ahead of its time." —David Piper

◉ Another close group of competitors enters Bottom Bend with Chris Craft (7) Lola leading the Norinder/Widdows (6) Lola and the Prophet/Nelson (12) Lola. Craft and Eric Liddell finished eighth and were the only Lola to finish in the top 10.

"I drove a Lola T70 coupe in 1969, and I think the first coupe that I drove was an older Mk.3 that had been sold off to my sponsor Tech-Speed by Sid Taylor. That car was bloody quick, but it was a compromise to the newer 3B that most of the others were racing at that time. That Lola was a lovely car, a wonderful car, and it was a lot of fun to drive. We got misled by a few people because we were new into it, and we got a lot of dummy information. That car was very good, and I think we embarrassed a few people occasionally. In our first meeting at Silverstone, we put that car on the pole, ahead of Denny in the brand new one. After we got that car sorted out, we won several races with it and beat a lot of good people. That Lola was a very successful car, and it was a shame that it was sold to McQueen's film company, because it was later crashed into the trees by radio control, disguised as a Ferrari. That was a very sad demise to a bloody good car. We won the Wills Trophy at Croft and the Martini International Trophy at Silverstone, both big international meetings, in that car. Those meetings are among the happiest memories of my racing days." —Chris Craft

◉ The Bonnier/Muller Lola appeared at the Targa Florio in May 1969 and ran as high as third place before a lost wheel put them on the sideline.

◉ The start of the 1,000 km at Spa saw the Hawkins/Prophet/Piper Lola T70 Mk.3B lead a huge starting field through Eue Rouge. Behind Hawkins are Ickx/Oliver (1) Gulf Mirage, Rodriguez/Piper/Amon (8) Ferrari 312P, Siffert/Redman (25) Porsche 908, Bonnier/Muller (32) Lola T70 Mk.3B, Elford/Aherns/Attwood (10) Porsche 908, the Pilette/Slotemaker (16) Alfa Romeo, and the rest of the field. Hawkins led the race for a while but lost his engine, and the Bonnier/Muller Lola finished fifth overall and won the Group 4 class.

◉ David Piper finished third at Dijon in May 1969.

"When I got my first T70 [it was one of the first four or five Mk.3B coupes built], you had to have a car that the manufacturer had produced 50 of to be eligible to run any engine over 3 liters in the world championship. We were in a desperate state because we had the Ferrari P3 and it was a good car, but we could only run it in prototype racing. We ran quite a few prototype races on the continent, but we didn't have any place to go in the World Championship races. Suddenly, the only cars that were eligible for the championship were the Ford GT40, which got a second lease on life, and the Lola T70. I wanted something different so I went to see Peter Agg about getting an M6 McLaren coupe, but they couldn't promise any type of delivery so I finally settled on a T70. I was quite friendly with Grand Prix driver Jo Bonnier who was the Lola agent in Europe at that time. In those days, the Formula 1 drivers were just as keen to drive the sports cars as they were to drive their F1 cars. Funny enough, I used to deliver all of the Lolas from Lola Cars to Bonnier's place in Switzerland, and Jo invited me to be the sports car representative in the GPDA [Grand Prix Driver's Association]." —David Piper

The Bonnier/Muller Lola makes a nose-down landing at the Nürburgring in June 1969. This car went out of the race with a broken driveshaft after 23 of 44 laps.

◉ Only one Lola started at Le Mans in 1969, and that was driven by Jo Bonnier, Masten Gregory, and Herbert Muller. The Lola ran as high as sixth place before a blown engine in the 13th hour ended any chance of a well-placed finish.

◉ Once again, only one Lola showed up at the July 1969 Watkins Glen 6-Hour Race, and it was driven by Jo Bonnier, Chuck Parsons, and Herbert Muller. The Siffert/Redman (1) Porsche 908 leads the field away from the start. Behind the Porsche is the Servoz-Gavin/Rodriguez (9) Matra M650, Elford/Attwood (4) Porsche 908, Bonnier/Muller (11) Lola T70 Mk.3B, and the Buzzetta/Lins (2) Porsche 908. The Lola lost an engine after 165 laps and did not finish.

◉ One of the most interesting things about the Watkins Glen Can-Am was that it was run the day after the 6-Hour Race. This allowed any of the previous day's competitors to compete with the big boys, and it made for some very interesting and varied starting fields. It also made for some surprising result sheets at the end of the day. Jo Bonnier (19) Lola T70 Mk.3B laps Fred Baker (29) McLaren M6B on his way to a seventh-place finish in the Can-Am race.

◉ The Lola's proudest moment in 1969 happened at the Osterreichring 1,000 km in August. Jo Bonnier (33) Lola T70 Mk.3B is first off the line ahead of Ickx/Oliver (9) Gulf Mirage, Siffert/Aherns (29) Porsche 917, Servoz-Gavin/Rodriguez (42) Matra M650, Giunti/Galli (6) Alfa Romeo 33/3, Attwood/Redman (30) Porsche 917, Gregory/Brostrom (11) Porsche 908/2, and the rest of the field. This race illustrated the difference in aerodynamics between the new 917 and the Lola, as the Bonnier/Muller Lola fought it out with the two 917s for the overall win. When the race ended, the Siffert/Aherns 917 was the winner by 67 seconds, but the Bonnier/Muller Lola finished on the same lap and ahead of the second 917. David Piper drove a Lola in the race, but he also owned the third-place 917. Piper and Frank Gardner had driven the 917 at the Nürburgring in May, but Piper opted for the lesser of two evils at Osterreichring.

"The T70 was much better aerodynamically than the original Porsche 917. Frank Gardner and I drove the 917 the first time that it was ever raced at the Nürburgring. In 1969, Porsche was having tremendous problems with the 917 lifting off of the ground. The tail section was like a wing, and it was causing the car to lift off of the ground. Out of the slow corners at the Nürburgring, you had a lot of squat so that you had a lot of negative camber, and the car would accelerate out of the corners well. But when you went faster, the back of the car lifted off of the ground and you went on positive camber. That made the car very difficult to drive because you were suddenly sucked off of the ground. What that Porsche needed was a good spoiler on the back. I remember that after the race Jurgen Barth and all of the Porsche people were all over my T70 that I had brought to the Nürburgring just in case, wondering how the suspension geometry worked. They just couldn't come to terms with the fact that they had gotten all of their bodywork wrong. In the end, when we put a flat deck on the back of the 917 that was similar to the deck on the Lola T70, the 917 was immediately seconds quicker." —David Piper

"I drove the first 917 that was raced at the Nürburgring in 1969. You didn't drive that beast, you hung on to it. You were a high-speed passenger looking for support in that car." —Frank Gardner

◉ One of the most anticipated events of the 1969 Can-Am season was the arrival of the long-rumored Penske Sunoco Lola T163. The Lola, with Mark Donohue driving, finally showed up at Mid Ohio, five races into the 11-race season. Donohue (6) qualified third fastest in spite of half-shaft and engine problems. Also on the starting grid are Chuck Parsons (10) Lola T163, John Surtees (7) Chaparral 2H, George Eaton (98) McLaren M12, Jo Siffert (0) Porsche 917PA, Peter Revson (31) Lola T163, and Lothar Motschenbacher (11) McLaren M12. Donohue broke another half-shaft eight laps into the race, and the big blue Lola was driven off into the sunset never to return.

◉ Chuck Parsons' Lola T163 had sprouted a wing by the time the Can-Am series had moved to Laguna Seca in October. Parsons, on his way to a third-place finish, leads Tony Dean (9) Porsche 908 and Mario Andretti (1) McLaren M6B into Turn 9. Parsons was always the highest placed Lola in the 1969 Can-Am final results, and he finished third in the championship.

Peter Revson (31) Lola T163 was the second-best Lola in the 1969 Can-Am series, finishing 11th in the final championship standings. Revson's highest placing was a fourth at Road America. At Riverside, Revson laps Bruce Campbell (9) BVC Mk.1.

◉ The Brian Redman/John Love (1) Lola T70 Mk.3B took the pole position ahead of a very strong field at the Kyalami 9-Hour Race. For this race, the Sid Taylor car was painted in the Team Gunston colors. Unfortunately, the Lola went out of the race with engine and rear-end problems. In late 1970, this Lola was bought by Mike Coombe to race in England and on the continent in 1971.

"That Lola coupe was a lovely car to drive and a beautiful car to look at. I drove it in the 1971 long-distance races and in the Interserie, which was being run on the Continent at the time. I co-drove with Paul Vestey, who had driven Ferraris and Porsches. By 1971, the Lola was a bit over the hill compared to the Porsche 917s and the Ferrari 512s that we were up against. In those days, we were all in it for the fun, and we didn't take the placings so seriously. I got on reasonably well in the Interserie, but we didn't do anything startling. Our car was originally purchased by Sid Taylor in 1969, and he raced it with Hamilyn Books sponsorship. The Lola was white with a green stripe over the top of it. It was driven by Frank Gardner, Brian Redman, and Denny Hulme, amongst others. The car was driven mostly in the British Series, which was quite strong then. We had an endless number of great races in the UK in those days. In 1970, the car was bought by Team Gunston in South Africa, and it was raced in the Springbok Series by John Love. I bought the car from Paul Vestey who had brought the car back to the UK, and we raced it during the 1971 season. We had a quite trouble-free season with the car because it was reliable, and it was, at that time, a good amateur's car. We had a Bartz Chevrolet engine in the Lola, and it was detuned for reliability. After the 1971 season, I sold it and it became a road car." —Mike Coombe

◉ By 1970, this was the only Lola T70 Mk.3B that attempted to run at Daytona and Sebring. With the coming of the Ferrari 512s, Porsche 917s, Alfa Romeo 33/3s, and the Matra MS650s, it was painfully obvious that the Lola was a museum relic and that it would soon fade into history. Drivers John Cannon, George Eaton, Bob Brown, Gregg Young, and Robin Ormes made a gallant attempt at both races, but the results were the same: DNF.

○ The de Udy/Gardner (7) Lola leads the De Cadenet/Del Rio Porsche 908/2 over the rain-swept Brands Hatch circuit in April 1970. The Lola blew an engine, and the Porsche lost a gearbox.

"I drove Sid Taylor's Lolas a few times, and I drove both the open and closed cars for him. I also drove the coupe that belonged to Mike de Udy. The T70 Lola was the best car of that era, and it was a good safe motor car. It never gave you the spooky feeling that it would get airborne; it was never twitchy, it had good brakes, and the Chevrolet engine was much better than the Ford. The general package was a very good one, and Eric Broadley did a fair old job on that car, and it was probably one of his better efforts. In a straight line, that coupe was aerodynamically pretty slippery. One of the best and most comfortable things about that car was that the fuel tanks had bladders in them. That was a pleasant relief after driving open-wheelers that had aluminum fuel tanks on either side of you, a tank on top of your family jewels, and a tank under your ass. The Lolas were quite civilized, and everything on those cars was quite functional. Eric Broadley had a fair amount of experience with his GT car and the GT40s, and I think, he really tidied up all of the mistakes that were made in those cars. Eric had learned a lot from the GT40 exercise, and the T70 featured all of the good things that he had learned. The Lola was very well engineered, and it wasn't a bad car to work on. It had a good monocoque chassis that gave you confidence that you could walk away from if you had an accident. It was the first of the safer-era motor cars, and the car was very good in both the wet and the dry."
—Frank Gardner

○ Teddy Pilette and Taf Gosselin (16) lead the Koch/Dechent (44) Porsche 908/2 and the Rodriguez/Kinnunen (7) Porsche 917K at the Monza 1,000 km. The Lola finished 16th overall and 10th in class.

◉ At Spa, the Bonnier/Wisell (33) Lola finished 10th overall after running as high as seventh early in the race—not a bad result for an outdated car running against a lot of very stiff competition.

◉ The Pilette/Gosselin (35) Lola was as high as fourth overall at Spa before suspension problems put them out of the race.

When the 1970 Can-Am series began at Mosport in June, Lola debuted a brand new car dubbed the T220 with Peter Revson as the driver. The car was very fast in a straight line but suffered handling problems because of its short (88-inch) wheelbase. The T220, designed and constructed by Eric Broadley and Bob Marston, featured an aluminum alloy monocoque chassis and a 465-cubic-inch aluminum alloy engine. Peter Revson (26) Lola T220 leads Bob Brown (3) McLeagle at St. Jovite. Revson retired soon after with a blown engine, and Brown finished fourth overall.

◉ At St. Jovite, Chuck Parsons (19) Lola T163 is closely pursued by George Eaton (98) BRM P154. Parsons finished eighth, while Eaton finished third.

◉ Peter Revson on the gas at Edmonton. Unfortunately, an oil leak put him out of the race.

◉ Peter Revson (26) Lola T220 and Chris Amon (77) March 707 battle for third and fourth position at Laguna Seca. Revson and Amon finished in this order with Revson taking third place and Amon finishing fourth. The Lola T220 that Revson was driving here was a longer-wheelbase (98 inches) car than the one in which he started the season. The handling and Revson's results improved dramatically with this new car.

Ⓒ Bob Bondurant (21) drove this much-modified Lola T160 during the 1970 Can-Am season. Bondurant, leading Pedro Rodriguez (1) BRM 154 at Laguna Seca, had only one finish during the season, a second place at Road America.

CHAPTER 4

FADE TO BLACK
1971-1974

Could anyone break McLaren's four-year domination of the Can-Am series? Several people had tried, or threatened to, but it was Eric Broadley who, in 1971, really stepped up to the plate and offered a legitimate contender with a package consisting of the Lola T260 and Jackie Stewart as driver.

The T260 was Lola's most serious Can-Am effort since 1966, an all-new car from the ground up. When the series opened at Mosport in June, Stewart immediately put the T260 on the pole, almost a full second ahead of the two Team McLaren M8Fs. Two weeks later, Stewart qualified second and won the race at St. Jovite. After St. Jovite, most people associated with the Can-Am felt that Stewart had a real chance to unseat the McLaren duo for the year-end championship. It was not to be, however. Except for another win at Mid-Ohio and two second-place finishes at Edmonton and Laguna Seca, the season quickly went to hell as various mechanical problems plagued the Lola effort. One of the biggest problems the T260 had was keeping its front end on the ground. Even the addition of a "cow catcher"-type wing on the front and movement of the rear spoiler farther back on the rear deck didn't seem to cure the problem. Stewart finished the 10-race season with two wins and two second places, but it wasn't near enough to prevent Peter Revson of McLaren from becoming the first American Can-Am Champion. Stewart finished third in the year-end championship.

The T70-based Lola coupes appeared in several European events in 1971 and 1972, but they were completely outdistanced by newer and more sophisticated machinery from Porsche, Matra, and Alfa Romeo.

Lola made its final attempt at Can-Am glory in 1972 with the Lola T310. One of the biggest problems for all of the competitors, including McLaren, in 1972 was the arrival of the turbo Porsches. The 310 did not arrive for the first race at Mosport, but when the car did arrive for the second race of the year at Road Atlanta, David Hobbs was not at all impressed. Nothing seemed to work properly, and Hobbs hated the car. The T310's best finish was a fourth place at Watkins Glen.

At the end of the 1972 season, both Lola and McLaren withdrew from any further factory participation in the Can-Am series. By the time the 1973 season started, most of the Lolas that were on the grid were at least two years old, and they were well outpaced by the Porsche 917/30KL, numerous Porsche 917/10Ks, and the two Shadow DN2s.

By 1974, the Can-Am was dead and the only factory participation came from the Shadow team. The rest of the field was made up of older cars, and the best of the Lolas were the two 1971 model T260s driven by Bob Nagel and John Gunn. Nagel was the top finishing Lola driver at year's end in both 1973 and 1974. When the Can-Am died at Road America on August 25, 1974, Lola Cars Ltd. moved on to other ventures that brought the company the fame and fortune that had so long eluded it.

⊙ When the Can-Am season opened at Mosport in June 1971, excitement reigned supreme because Lola Cars Ltd. had finally unveiled a car (Lola T260) that could, and would, challenge the dominant McLaren team. This radically shaped car, powered by a 494-cubic-inch aluminum Chevrolet engine built by George Foltz and driven by Jackie Stewart, gave the McLaren team fits when it ran properly. At Mosport, the T260 qualified for the pole and was almost a full second faster than the factory McLarens. In the race, Stewart was leading the McLaren of Denny Hulme when the transaxle failed and put him out of the race. At St. Jovite (pictured here), Denny Hulme's McLaren M8F took the pole, but Stewart came from second starting position to win the race, beating both team McLarens (Denny Hulme and Peter Revson) in the process.

Only one Lola (5) appeared at Le Mans in June 1971, and that car was driven by Teddy Pilette and Taf Gosselin. The Lola ran as high as third place before exiting the race in the ninth hour with gearbox problems.

Hiroshi Kazato (88) Lola T222 (production version of previous year's T220) finished in sixth place at St. Jovite and became the first Japanese driver to finish in the top 10 in a Can-Am race.

Ⓐ Jackie Stewart established himself and the Lola T260 as serious challengers for the 1971 Can-Am championship with his convincing win at St. Jovite.

Saying that Jackie Stewart's win at St. Jovite was a popular one with the fans would be a gross understatement.

◉ Bob Nagel (16) Lola T222 was one of the very few privateers who ran a Lola in the 1971 Can-Am series. At Road Atlanta, Nagel leads Roger McCraig (55) McLaren M8E and Denny Hulme (5) McLaren M8F before leaving the race with overheating problems.

◉ By the time the Can-Am series moved to Laguna Seca in October, many modifications had been made to the T260 in an attempt to improve the less-than-desirable handling characteristics. The rear wing was moved farther up on the car, and a snowplow-type spoiler was added to the nose. It helped, but Jackie Stewart recently stated that this was one of the worst-handling cars that he had ever driven.

Jackie Stewart (1) Lola T260 and David Hobbs (49) TI22 Mk. II race side by side down the corkscrew at Laguna Seca. Jackie Oliver (101) Shadow Mk.2 and Brian Redman (38) BRM P167 are on the hill behind. Stewart finished second overall, and Hobbs went out of the race with starter problems.

▶ Frustration in the pits as adjustments are made to try and improve the performance and handling of Lola's 1972 Can-Am entry, the Lola T310.

"The Lola T310 that I drove in the 1972 Can-Am series was the worst car that Eric ever built. Driving that car was an absolutely dreadful experience. That was one of those strange deals where Frank Gardner did all of the testing in England, and I did all of the standing around. I never got any time in the car before we went to Road Atlanta for the second race of the season. During practice, the wheel came off on the downhill straight at about 180 miles per hour. That was my first experience with that car, and it never got any better." —David Hobbs

◉ David Hobbs had his best finish (fourth) of the season at Watkins Glen in July.

◉ Reine Wisell drove one of the Lola T260s at Watkins Glen. This was Wisell's only appearance in a Can-Am car. To control front-end lift, note how far the wing extends from the front of the car, leaving one to wonder whether the car is trying to imitate (a) a steam locomotive with a big cow catcher, or (b) a snowplow getting ready for the upcoming upstate New York ski season. Wisell blew the engine on the 19th lap.

Early in the race at Watkins Glen, David Hobbs (1) Lola T310 leads Jackie Oliver (101) Shadow Mk.3 and George Follmer (6) Porsche 917/10K. Hobbs finished fourth, Follmer finished fifth, and Oliver crashed.

"I had some semi-reasonable results that year with the T310, but I was always about three seconds a lap off the pace, and it never got any better. I made a major career error when Roger Penske asked me to stand in for Mark Donohue, who had had a huge practice crash at Atlanta, and I said no because I felt an obligation to drive the Lola. Of course, Roger hired George Follmer, and he won the championship going away. I can truly say that I drove the best car that Eric ever built [T70] and the worst one that he ever built [T310]."
—David Hobbs

By the time David Hobbs raced the T310 at Laguna Seca, a new front body section had been installed. It was better, but not good enough, and sadly the Lola factory effort would pass into history after the final 1972 race at Riverside. Hobbs races to an eighth-place finish as Lothar Motschenbacher (11) McLaren M8D and Sam Posey (20) Porsche 917PA follow. Motschenbacher finished 11th, and Posey finished 5th.

154

There were a fair number (6) of Lolas that showed up at Laguna Seca for the Can-Am race. Tom Heyser (61) Lola T260, about to be lapped by Mark Donohue, finished ninth.

Bob Nagel (17) Lola T222 leads Lothar Motschenbacher (11) McLaren M8D on his way to a 14th-place finish at Laguna Seca.

The highest-placing Lola at Laguna Seca was the T222 of Charlie Kemp who finished sixth.

At Riverside, Tom Heyser passes Frank Kahlich (30) McLaren M12 on the inside of Turn 6. Heyser finished 19th and Kahlich finished 11th.

By the time the 1973 Can-Am season opened, most of the Lolas from seasons past had been parked. Tom Heyser continued to campaign his two-year-old T260 and had a fine eighth place at Watkins Glen to show for it.

⊙ Bob Nagel also chose to keep racing his outdated T260 in 1973, and his consistent finishing record gave him an excellent fifth place in the final 1973 championship standings. Nagel also came back for the 1974 season with the same car and finished fourth in the abbreviated season's final championship standings.

EPILOGUE

What happened to the very successful Lola Group 7 and Can-Am effort of 1965 and 1966, and why did it lose steam when it was at the top of the heap? I think a major reason can be summed up in one word: Indianapolis. In May 1965, two Lola T80s appeared at the Indianapolis Motor Speedway and were qualified for the 500-mile race by Al Unser Sr. and Bud Tingelstad. Unser finished ninth, and Tingelstad was running in fifth when a wheel broke on the 116th lap and put him into the wall. Lola returned to the speedway in 1966 with two new cars (the T90) and drivers Jackie Stewart and Graham Hill. Famed two-time Indianapolis 500 winner Rodger Ward also drove one of the year-old Lolas in the race. Jackie Stewart led most of the last 100 miles, but he was put out of the race with oil pressure problems with eight laps to go. Graham Hill went on to score Lola's first of three Indianapolis wins in only the company's second year of oval-track competition. Rodger Ward finished 15th in his final race at Indianapolis before his retirement.

In 1967, Lola had three cars in the 500. Al Unser Sr. finished second in a new car, and Chuck Hulse finished seventh in a year-old car. The third car, for Jackie Stewart, blew an engine on lap 169 while running in third place.

Also during this time John Surtees, now driving for Honda's F1 program, asked Eric Broadley and his team to develop a proper chassis for the Honda engine. This was done, and Surtees won the Italian Grand Prix with the Lola-Honda in 1967. Lola and Honda also worked together on the 1968 car. About this time Lola also started to get involved with F5000, and its cars came to dominate that series for several years. Lola also built several under- and over-2.0-liter Group 6 cars (T210, T212, T280, T282, T292, and T294) that raced successfully in endurance races in Europe and North America throughout the 1970s.

I believe the demise of Lola's interest in the Can-Am can be attributed to a simple case of too much going on at the same time. The Can-Am and sports car racing programs lost out to more profitable projects. Following the demise of the Can-Am in 1974, Lola became involved in the restructured Can-Am series and dominated those races from 1977 to 1981 with drivers Patrick Tambay, Jacky Ickx, and Geoff Brabham. In 1978, Lola returned to its winning ways in Indy car racing with the successful T500. Al Unser Sr. won the second Indianapolis 500 for Lola and also won the 1978 Triple Crown, which consisted of the three 500-mile races at Indy, Pocono, and Ontario.

Starting in 1983, Lola dominated Indy car racing through the end of the 1996 season. During the period from 1965 to 1996, Lola won three Indianapolis 500s, 105 championship races, 74 pole positions, and 6 manufacturers championships.

Lola's fortunes turned in 1997, however, with an ill-fated entry into Formula 1. That ill-advised project almost caused terminal financial difficulties for the company, and those difficulties were magnified even more by the failure of the T97/00 chassis in the Championship Auto Racing Teams (CART) series. It is hoped the Lola Cars Ltd. will find its way back to past glories with the new management team and a new name, Lola Cars International Ltd.

INDEX

Agapiou, Charlie, 122
Amon, Chris, 11, 54, 61, 66–68, 108, 131, 142
Andretti, Mario, 70, 99, 118, 136
Arkus-Duntov, Zora, 24
Attwood, Richard, 20–22, 37, 105, 131, 133, 135
Bahamas Speed Week, 71
Baker, Fred, 29, 133
Beresford, Don, 14
Bianchi, Lucien, 23
Bianchi, Mauro, 113
Bignotti, George, 51
BOAC 500, 83, 129, 130
Bondurant, Bob, 41, 42, 49–51, 74, 143
Bonnier, Jo, 93, 104, 105, 108, 113, 115–117, 125, 129–133, 135, 140
Brabham, Geoff, 159
Brabham, Jack, 38, 52
Bridgehampton USRRC Can-Am, 61, 81, 86, 99, 118
Broadley, Eric, 11, 12, 15, 19, 20, 34, 37, 39, 93, 98, 141, 145, 159
Brown, Bob, 138, 141
Bucher, Bob, 55
Bucknum, Ronnie, 107, 128
Burness, Bruce, 74, 101
Butler, George, 11
Butler, Gordon, 11
Campbell, Bruce, 137
Cannon, John, 37, 41, 42, 55, 81, 138
Casner, Lucky, 23
Charles, Maurice, 23
Clark, Jim, 39, 43, 44
Collins, John, 104
Coombe, Mike, 138
Cordts, John, 120
Coundley, John, 32, 52, 54
Craft, Chris, 93, 117, 130
Daytona, 105–107
de Udy, Mike, 84, 90, 93, 113, 117, 122, 139
Dean, Tony, 108, 136
Dibley, Hugh P. K., 37, 43, 50, 52, 54, 58, 77, 90, 98, 100, 113
Doane, Dick, 31
Donohue, Mark, 37, 38, 45, 55–57, 64, 66, 68, 70, 71, 73, 74, 76, 81, 82, 85, 86, 88, 100–102, 105, 107, 127, 136, 155
Durst, Steve, 111
Dutch Grand Prix, 11
Eaton, George, 108, 136, 138, 142
Edmonton Can-Am race, 105, 120, 142
Elford, Vic, 105, 111, 113, 131, 133
Entin, Jerry, 121
Epstein, Jackie, 77, 104, 115, 120, 121
Eve, Bill, 55
Everly, John, 25
Foitek, Karl, 113
Follmer, George, 38, 66, 73–76, 81, 85, 86, 88, 94, 101, 122, 154
Fowler, Bill, 65
Foyt, A. J., 38, 51, 67, 70
Fulp, John "Buck," 55, 57, 70, 71
Gammino, Mike, 25
Gardner, Frank, 52, 90, 93, 114, 122, 135, 139
Garner, Jim, 103, 126

Gates, Charlie, 31
Ginther, Richie, 41
Gosselin, Gustave, 109
Gosselin, Taf, 139, 140, 146
Goth, Mike, 55, 68, 74, 76
Grand Prix for Sports Cars, 49, 50
Grant, Jerry, 38, 49, 51, 53, 55, 56, 63, 74, 76
Gregory, Masten, 133, 135
Grossman, Bob, 41
Guards Trophy race, 23, 32, 44, 98, 121
Guldstrand, Dick, 113
Gunn, John, 105, 112, 145
Gurney, Dan, 37, 38, 42, 58, 61, 65, 66, 86–89, 99, 122
Haas, Carl, 104, 116
Hall, Jim, 11, 25, 27, 41–43, 49, 86, 88, 89, 90, 97
Hamill, Ed, 55
Hansgen, Walt, 29, 31, 33, 37, 44, 45, 48, 49, 51, 91
Harris, Trevor, 74
Hawkins, Paul, 37, 58, 77, 83, 90, 108, 117, 129–131
Hayes, Charlie, 46, 51, 88, 120
Heyser, Tom, 155, 157
Hill, Graham, 49, 159
Hill, Phil, 64, 85
Hissom, Ronnie, 41, 42
Hitchcock, Tommy, 23
Hobbs, David, 12, 19, 22, 37, 43, 44, 46, 78, 79, 84, 85, 98, 102, 105, 111, 113, 145, 151–154
Hudson, Skip, 57
Hugus, Ed, 41, 42
Hulme, Denny, 38, 52, 54, 67, 88, 90, 93, 114, 116, 129, 149
Hulse, Chuck, 159
Ickx, Jacky, 79, 113, 131, 135, 159
Indianapolis Motor Speedway, 159
International Trophy Race, 37, 54
Ireland, Innes, 23
Jackson, Peter, 20
Johnson, Delmo, 41, 42
Johnson, Samuel C., 69
Jones, Parnelli, 37, 49–51, 59, 66, 67, 88–90, 100
Jordan, Dave, 103, 105, 113, 128
Kahlich, Frank, 157
Kainhofer, Karl, 56, 57, 102
Kazato, Hiroshi, 146
Kelly, Max, 99
Kemp, Charlie, 111, 156
Kent, Washington, USRRC, 57
Kerrison, R. C., 23
Kolb, Charlie, 76
Krause, Bill, 52
Kronn, Mak, 55
Kumnick, Roy, 31
Kwech, Horst, 113
Laguna Seca Can-Am race, 48, 65, 66, 76, 111, 116, 121, 136, 142, 143, 149, 154–156
Lance, Frank, 24, 28, 30, 32, 51
Las Vegas USRRC Can-Am race, 52, 69, 73, 90, 91, 122
Le Mans, 19, 20, 72, 78, 79, 102, 104, 109, 120, 133, 146

Leslie, Ed, 41, 96, 105–107, 113, 121, 125, 128
Liddell, Eric, 115, 130
Lola Models
    Formula Junior, 11
    Mk. 1, 11
    Mk. 6 GT Coupe, 10–35
    T70, 36–91, 94, 96–98, 100, 116, 121, 122
    T70 Mk. 3, 38, 100
    T70 Mk.3B, 38, 124, 138
    T160, 94–96, 118–120
    T162, 123
    T163, 94, 136
    T210, 150
    T212, 159
    T220, 94, 141, 142
    T222, 146, 149, 156
    T260, 110, 112, 145, 147, 149, 157, 158
    T280, 159
    T282, 159
    T292, 159
    T294, 159
    T310, 145, 152, 154
    T500, 159
Los Angeles Times Grand Prix, 12, 34, 35, 49, 68, 99, 100
Love, John, 138
Maggs, Tony, 14–18
Mallone, Malcolm, 65, 68
Marston, Bob, 141
McCluskey, Roger, 71, 103
McCraig, Roger, 149
McKay, Walt, 43
McLaren, Bruce, 23, 43, 49, 54, 59–61, 86, 88–90, 99
Mecom, John, 12, 23–25, 30, 37, 49, 59, 98
Miles, Ken, 41
Mitter, Gerhard, 105, 113
Monza 1,000 km, 139
Morley, Bud, 74
Moser, Silvio, 41
Mosport Can-Am race, 47, 63, 64, 98
Moss, Stirling, 69
Motschenbacher, Lothar, 74, 76, 81, 88, 103, 105–107, 125, 126, 128, 136, 154, 155
Muller, Herbert, 129–133
Nagel, Bob, 93, 11, 112, 145, 149, 155, 158
Nassau Tourist Trophy Race, 11, 25–27, 28, 51, 70, 71
Neerpasch, Jochen, 15
Nelson, Edward, 104, 120, 121, 130
Nürburgring 1,000 Km, 14–18, 78, 102, 132
Oliver, Jackie, 93, 121, 131, 135, 151, 154
Olthoff, Bob, 16–18
Ormes, Robin, 138
Osterreichring 1,000 km, 135
Oulton Park Tourist Trophy, 43, 52
Pabst, Augie, 8, 9, 11, 12, 23, 25–35, 97
Parnell, Reg, 11
Parsons, Chuck, 51, 55, 73, 81, 88, 93, 94, 104, 105, 107, 108, 115, 116, 119, 127, 133, 136, 142
Patrick, Scooter, 100, 103, 105, 113, 128

Penske, Roger, 25, 64, 82, 127
Pierpoint, Roy, 37, 50, 90, 129
Pilette, Teddy, 109, 131, 139, 140, 146
Piper, David, 44, 46, 52, 85, 93, 108, 121, 129, 130, 131, 135
Player's 200, 30, 43, 46, 97
Posey, Sam, 70, 81, 94, 105, 119, 120, 154
Pretorius, Jackie, 90
Prophet, David, 84, 108, 130, 131
Racing Car Show, 11, 12, 38, 71, 123
Rand Daily Mail 9-Hour Endurance Race at Kyalami, 50, 122, 138
Redman, Brian, 37, 38, 52, 54, 93, 105, 114, 129, 131, 133, 135, 138, 151
Revson, Peter, 70, 73, 74, 76, 81, 88, 90, 94, 103, 104, 110, 129, 130, 136, 137, 141, 142, 145
Rey, Jacques, 109
Riley, Art, 25
Riverside USRRC Can-Am race, 35, 68, 74, 89, 93, 99, 108, 109, 137, 154, 157
Road America 500, 33, 34, 45, 57, 85, 97, 118
Road America June Sprints, 30, 31
Road Atlanta, 149
Rodriguez, Pedro, 41, 42, 105, 131, 133, 135, 139, 143
Rushbrook, Rob, 14
Salvadori, Roy, 11, 22
Sargent, Peter, 23
Savage, Swede, 94, 105, 122
Scott, Skip, 67, 70, 73, 74, 76, 104, 105, 116
Sebring, 12 Hours of, 28, 41, 42, 71, 96, 107, 128
Senior Service 200, 39
Serrurier, Doug, 50, 90
Sharp, Hap, 31, 47, 49, 51, 70
Siffert, Jo, 105, 131, 133, 135, 136
Silverstone International Daily Express Trophy, 14
Silverstone Players Trophy Race, 114
Spa Francorchamps 1,000 km, 77, 108, 115, 131, 140
Speedworld International Trophy race, 117
Spence, Mike, 85, 88, 90
St. Jovite, 58–60, 141, 142, 145–148
Stardust Grand Prix, 51
Stewart, Jackie, 37, 47, 65, 99, 110, 145, 147–149, 151, 159
Surtees, John, 9, 11, 14, 23, 37–39, 43–46, 58–60, 63, 67–69, 72, 78, 79, 83–86, 88, 91, 96–99, 102, 118, 120, 136, 159
Sutcliffe, Peter, 23, 84
Tambay, Patrick, 159
Targa Florio, 77, 130
Taylor, Sidney, 52, 67, 114
Thompson, Dick, 11, 25, 27
Tingelstad, Bud, 159
Titus, Jerry, 120
Turckheim-Trios Epis hillclimb, 109
Unser, Al, Sr., 159
Ward, Rodger, 159
Watkins Glen USRRC race, 55, 56, 81, 104, 111, 112, 115, 116, 133, 153, 154, 157
Wisell, Reine, 140, 153
Young, Gregg, 138